Praise for *Renewing the Process of Creation:*
A Jewish Integration of Science and Spirit

"Compelling.... I invite both scholars in the interfaith conversation in faith and science and lay folks who recognize its crucial importance to read and ponder this engaging, provocative and inspiring book."
> —**Robert John Russell**, Ian G. Barbour Professor of Theology and Science in Residence, Graduate Theological Union

"That rare book that honors the scientific process and the scientific way of thinking, and, at the same time, celebrates the power and inspiration of religious living.... A deeply important book that will create more productive conversations and more sophisticated perspectives surrounding religion and science."
> —**Rabbi Geoffrey A. Mitelman**, founding director, Sinai and Synapses

"To show that a deeply Jewish understanding of God's 'evolving, emergent, dynamic creation' is fully compatible with today's science, and that Jewish reflections on human nature resonate with emergent evolution—well, that would really be an achievement. You're holding that achievement in your hands."
> —**Dr. Philip Clayton**, editor, *The Oxford Handbook of Religion and Science*; Ingraham Professor, Claremont School of Theology

"Deeply intellectually satisfying.... Articulates a winsome interface between that dynamism of creation and the patterned dynamism of Jewish liturgical life. [Rabbi Artson's] capacity to link scientific understanding to the cadences of Jewish faith is a compelling and welcome read."
> —**Dr. Walter Brueggemann**, Columbia Theological Seminary

"Explains recent scientific developments in accessible ways and then mines them for theological significance, powerfully making the case for an integration of science and religion that offers both metaphysical meaning and a plan for action. Modeling the commitment to process that he espouses, Artson's *Renewing the Process of Creation* draws richly on the Jewish past while pointing toward—and so helping to create—an affirmative future."

—**Rabbi Deborah Waxman, PhD**, president, Reconstructionist Rabbinical College and Jewish Reconstructionist Communities

"This book does something new and long overdue: it brings together Judaism, modern cosmology and Process Theology. Rabbi Artson is poetic, insightful and articulate, and his book is rich in spiritual and ethical conclusions. I was excited to read it."

—**Dr. Howard Smith**, senior astrophysicist, Harvard-Smithsonian Center; author, *Let There Be Light: Modern Cosmology and Kabbalah, a New Conversation between Science and Religion*

"A festival of a book…. Addictively and accessibly readable, adventurously faithful to the scientific and to the biblical heritage, [it] guides us all—spiritual seekers and skeptics, congregations and classes—to a celebration of our shared, fragile and gorgeous creaturehood."

—**Catherine Keller**, professor of constructive theology, Drew University; author, *On the Mystery: Discerning Divinity in Process*

"Process Theology joins Jewish scholarship in a stimulating investigation of creation. Beautifully written, informative, lucid, eminently readable. Read it!"

—**Francisco J. Ayala, PhD**, Donald Bren Professor of Biological Sciences, University of California, Irvine

Renewing
the Process
of Creation

A Jewish Integration
of Science and Spirit

Rabbi Bradley Shavit Artson, DHL

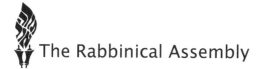

The Rabbinical Assembly

For People of All Faiths, All Backgrounds

JEWISH LIGHTS Publishing

Nashville, Tennessee

Renewing the Process of Creation:
A Jewish Integration of Science and Spirit

Grateful acknowledgment is given for permission to use the following: An earlier version of chapter 14 appeared in *Conservative Judaism* as "Embracing Death, Embracing the World: Our Alienation from Death and Creation," *Conservative Judaism* 48, no. 2 (Winter 1996): 49–54; an earlier version of the opening section of Part V was published in *Conservative Judaism* 44 (1991–1992): 25–35, and in *Judaism and Environmental Ethics: A Reader*, ed. Martin D. Yaffe (Lanham, MD: Lexington Books, 2001), 161–171. Both reprinted with permission of the Rabbinical Assembly. On page 125, Abraham ibn Ezra, translated and adapted by Rabbi Sidney Greenberg and Rabbi Jonathan D. Levine, cited in *A Garden of Choice Fruits: 200 Classic Jewish Quotes on Human Beings and the Environment*, ed. David E. Stein (Wyncote, PA: Shomrei Adamah, 1991), 66. Reprinted with permission.

Library of Congress Cataloging-in-Publication Data
Artson, Bradley Shavit, author.
  Renewing the process of creation : a Jewish integration of science and spirit / Rabbi Bradley Shavit Artson, DHL.
    pages cm
  Includes bibliographical references.
  ISBN 978-1-58023-833-5 (hardcover) — ISBN 978-1-58023-848-9 (ebook) — ISBN 978-1-68336-264-7 (paperback) 1. Jewish cosmology. 2. Human ecology—Religious aspects—Judaism. 3. Nature—Religious aspects—Judaism. 4. Creation—History of doctrines. 5. Judaism and science. I. Title.
  B157.C65A78 2015
  296.3'75—dc23
                    2015033948

10 9 8 7 6 5 4 3 2

Manufactured in the United States of America
Cover Design: Mike Myers
Cover Art: © agsandrew / Shutterstock

For People of All Faiths, All Backgrounds
Published by Jewish Lights Publishing
An Imprint of Turner Publishing Company
4507 Charlotte Avenue, Suite 100
Nashville, Tennessee 37209
Tel: (615) 255-2665
www.jewishlights.com

For my parents,
Barbara Friedman Artson
and
David Theodore Artson

and my grandparents,
Dorothy Berlin Friedman and Sydney Alexander Friedman
and
Minna Aptheker Artson and Matthew David Artson

with gratitude and love

Contents

Introduction
Creation in Process

In Your goodness, day after day, You renew creation.
U-ve-tuvo me-chadeish be-khol yom tamid ma'aseih vereishit.
—*Bereishit*[1]

Everything is creation in process.

We humans like to think of ourselves as in some way outside of creation, above nature, both for good and for ill. We flatter ourselves as the capstone of creation, the pinnacle of nature, and use our claimed rank as license for despoliation, entertainment, and distance, or we declare ourselves and our handiwork to be unnatural and artificial, binding ourselves with a "natural/unnatural" dichotomy that goads us toward either greater environmental awareness or disinterest. That misperception taints even our best efforts, and we cling to it so desperately—we need to be special, distinct, and superior. One wonders what insecurities drive such a desperate distortion. But we humans are not beyond nature. Rather, we are one of nature's blossoms; indeed, we are an instance of nature emerging as self-reflective consciousness. We are not above creation; we are one of its myriad manifestations. We did not appear, fully formed, divorced from the processes by which the cosmos emerged and generated every other form of becoming.

Indeed, the goal of this book will be to direct our awareness back to two rooted belongings: that humans and what we do are an integral part of the creation from which we emerge, which we embody, and which we impact. To develop this crucial insight requires a familiarity with the real world, that is to say, with contemporary scientific explanations of how the world actually works: what it's composed of, how those parts interact, how life emerges, how consciousness emerges out of life. So the book will begin by providing a common scientific literacy so that the thoughtful reader can proceed to deduce levels of meaning from what actually is, rather than from flights of imaginative fancy. Fleshing out a theology of creation in the light of science will allow us to articulate a deeper sense of space and time and our movement through both. Informed by science, this comprehensive narrative of the meaning of life and humanity will position the reader to express the ethical and moral implications of a creation theology, one that embraces earth as home, accepts humanity's role as steward and partner, and locates the constructive role of mortality and eternity within creation's embrace. Finally, the book will turn to the particular: how ancient Israel came to love all of earth by fostering a passion for a special place on the earth, how that recognition of land as holy enables a religious discipline of blessing and gratitude that makes it possible for life to blossom. In the end, the book will celebrate what it means to be mindful clay in a loving potter's grasp.

Creation is best understood not as a single event at a particular moment long, long ago, but as a continuous process that we express and in which we participate. Relating to creation as our context and home, participating in the process of continual creation, and recognizing divinity in the countless materializations of the cosmos and planet of which we are a part is the loam for everything else that emerges. The dynamics of all living is ongoing creation. All human development and, indeed, all human achievement occur within and as a manifestation of creation: revelation occurs within the context of creation; redemption and salvation are a consummation of creation.

Meaning Is Found within Relationships

What we know about creation is from our vantage point within creation, as the aspect of creation that is self-aware and articulate. We do not exist as disembodied minds or souls, seeking some point of contact with an external carnal reality. Culture does not erupt from some distillate of objective logic and bloodless thought. Instead, we recognize ourselves as biological creatures, embedded in biochemical interactions that are, themselves, constrained by the laws of physics. Our minds are emergent patterns of the very phenomenon we now seek to understand and articulate. Culture is the accumulated and remembered harvest of our embodied mental and emotional activities, shared across communities and distilled across generations. Knowing and reflecting upon creation, for our purposes, can best be addressed in stages of interrelating units: we need to assess what the sciences tell us about what the cosmos is and how it came to be, with special attention to our space-time bubble, our beloved third planet from the sun, life's biochemistry, and our human neuropsychology. While this factual knowledge cannot generate philosophical coherence by itself and presumes certain philosophical postulates to be visible at all, we require the discipline and clarity to organize what we know to then be able to address ourselves to what it means: How can we then integrate this knowing into enacting lives of meaning and participating in inclusive communities of justice, compassion, and love? How can we better love our people, all peoples, and ourselves? How can we extend that love to the other denizens of our aquamarine globe, to the earth itself, and to the cosmos as a whole?

From the first moments of human consciousness, people have sought to explain who we are, what we are to be doing, where we come from, and where we are headed. This urge to explain rests on a desire for coherence, predictability, and stability; to seek out reliable regularities—we abstract them into "laws" or "rules"—through which to comprehend the world and its ways and through which to fashion human societies and lives worth living. Expressive as we are of the broader creation, these very traits may provide evolutionary benefit and have been favored by natural selection. Whatever their proximate causes, human beings and our ancestors have been meaning seekers and meaning makers even before our most ancient beginnings. And at the start of that search are these questions: Why is there something rather than nothing? Why is the world comprehensible at all? Where did we come from? Do we belong?

Process Theology

That profoundly human quest has resulted in extraordinary endeavors through religion, art, and science to develop encompassing stories of the creation of the cosmos and our place in it and to force those disciplines to continue to converse and respond to each other. I categorize these modes of knowing beyond experience as the five M's: math, meditation, metaphor, music, myth.

For most of human history, myth, philosophy, and art were the dominant modes for locating ourselves in the cosmos and for setting our agenda, while science served a corroborating role to scripture. With the advent of modernity, that relationship shifted, as more and more of nature became susceptible to empirical testing and verifiable knowledge. Religion found itself retreating, staking its turf in the spots that science could not yet explain and then retreating again when new explanations became plausible. Still, religion, art, and science remain the tools humanity uses to explain itself in the world, to live with coherence and clarity, to concretize meaning and value. In our own time, we still crave a dynamic integration, harmony, and balance to make sense of our lives and to offer hope, with the caveat that science provides our generation with vastly more data than were available in previous times. Blinders and deliberate ignorance will not do; for any religion to claim plausibility, it must work within the information that sciences collect. No religious faith that flies in the face of scientific data can stand for long, nor should it.

There is a philosophical/religious school that takes the information of science as the best method for ascertaining physical reality.

What Process Thought then does is to attempt a speculative synthesis, a metaphysics, that integrates the latest scientific findings with deep-seated ethical and spiritual needs. Building on the insights of these scientific advances and the systemic speculation of a cluster of bold men and women—among them Henri Bergson, William James, Alfred North Whitehead, Charles Hartshorne, Mordecai Kaplan, Marjorie Suchocki, Milton Steinberg, John Cobb, Max Kadushin, Catherine Keller, Jay McDaniel, Patricia Farmer, and others—it is possible to comprehend the world as the dynamic, interrelating, self-determining dynamism it truly is.

For a comprehensive introduction to Process Thought and Theology with a Jewish perspective, the reader is invited to see my book *God of Becoming and Relationship: The Dynamic Nature of Process Theology* (Jewish Lights). In that book I offer a comprehensive overview of Process Thought, illustrated with examples taken from Jewish scripture and ethics. While reading *God of Becoming and Relationship* first would provide a context and background for the material covered in this book, it is not necessary; *Renewing the Process of Creation* stands on its own. In a similar vein, some basic scientific literacy would be helpful in following the discussion here, but I will provide background and examples so the interested reader will be able to acquire some scientific understanding as the reading proceeds.

Following is a brief summary of the key components of a Process worldview:

- The world and God are expressions of continuous, dynamic relational change. We label that process as creativity. The mutual commitment to that process is faithfulness (*emunah*), which rises above any faith (doctrine or creed).

- We and the world are not solid substances, but rather recurrent patterns of energy, occasions that change with each new instantiation but also maintain continuity from moment to moment. Think of the dynamic way electrons whir in quantum uncertainty, or how you are both different than you were ten years ago and also in significant ways the same person you've always been.

- We are interconnected, each to each and each to all. Our biology retains the story of where our ancestors have been and what they looked like, and our lives retain all our experiences and the ways others have had an impact on our choices, emotions, and temperament. We are who we are because of everyone we've known and because of our past, personal and ancestral. Therefore, all creation—not just humanity or a subset of humanity—has value and dignity.

- Every occasion has an interiority (first person mode, subjective) appropriate to its nature as well as an outer (third person, objective) way of related interaction and becoming. That is, we are all selves-in-relation. Think of the ways a baby intuits her parents, or a pet dog can sense fear or sorrow in its human companions. That intuitive link shapes our becoming in relation to everyone else.

- We and every occasion relate to each and all creation instantaneously and intuitively. We respond to the decisions of each other and of the totality, as we ourselves are re-created in each instant. Each new experience becomes a permanent part of our ongoing story and unfolding identity.

- God is the One who makes this relating possible, who creates the openness of a future of real novelty and the variety of its possibilities, and who relates to each of us in our particular individuality. That is to say, the future holds multiple possibilities that can be linked to our unchanging and single past. That very openness and pluralism is the gift of God, and an invitation for each of us to exercise our God-given capacity to choose our own future, to be self-determining.

- God is the One who invites us—and empowers us—in our particularity (hence, God knows us and relates to us as individuals) to select the optimal choice for our own flourishing (optimal in terms of maximizing experience, justice, compassion, and love) and for our mutual flourishing. Only you can determine whether to continue reading this book, to sign that petition, to volunteer with an inspiring cause. And you feel those choices as an expansive opportunity, while also discerning the best possible choice as a tug, a lure. To exist is to be self-determining, interconnected, and creative to some degree. Every event in nature—from an electron through an insect to a human—has the opportunity to exercise its self-determination, interconnection, and creativity at its own possible level.

- We and everything in the cosmos become co-creators with God in fashioning the present, which has primacy, out of the possibilities offered by the future and the constraints imposed by the past. God's primary mode of power is persuasive, not coercive. That goes for us, too. Our most impactful mentors were not those who could compel us against our will, but those who saw our potential and inspired us to make it actual: a great teacher, loving parent or grandparent, clergy, or friend.

- Once the present becomes actual, it is known eternally by God and cherished forever.

Process Thought recognizes that every aspect of the world is both self-determining and impacted by other self-determining aspects. Each becoming aspect, while retaining some consistency across time, is also engaged in dynamic integration of the world as it becomes something that generates novelty and greater connection. (For example, distant red giant stars created new elements such as carbon as they burned through their own fuel until the gravity was strong enough to collapse the stars in massive explosions, and much later shot them into the night sky. It is that very carbon that traveled all the way to the earth and makes life today possible.) Alfred North Whitehead, the preeminent founding Process thinker, described this becoming as "the many become one, and are increased by one."[2]

Rather than thinking of each becoming as a substance—unchanging, inert—Process Thought views each becoming as an event. With each new moment, each event is offered the range of potentialities made possible by its previous responses, the realities of the rest of the world around it, its history, and its own nature. Each event retains the capacity to respond from among the possibilities open to it at that moment, although one of those possibilities is the optimal choice in terms of love, compassion, relating, experience, and justice.

Process thinkers label that optimal choice "the lure." Like all great possibilities, it is not known rationally from the outside but is intuited from within. Alfred North Whitehead called that intuitive grasp "prehension." At each instant, we and all creation intuit the lure appropriate to our actual existence, and we retain the self-determination to strive for it or to reject it for other choices.

Two Rooted Belongings: Human and Natural

God, in the Process view, is the unifying ground that makes all relating possible and is the One who knows us from the inside and lures us and all creation in the direction of optimal development, experience, justice, and love rather than finding ourselves in an endless loop of meaningless repetition of the same natural laws. God is the One who meets us in our particularity and re-creates us as we choose a particular path, with that choice now ratified as a permanent part of our character and history. And God, knowing everything possible to know, retains our choices and our unique actuality forever.

In this understanding, God is not all-powerful in a coercive sense, but vastly, persistently powerful in a persuasive way. God does not, and cannot, break the rules. God works in, with, and through us (and all of creation) to advance the vision of a creation of greater relating and caring. We retain our freedom, like God, to be self-surpassing and to choose, within the constraints of our actuality, our next choice (that means I will never be a world-class ballet dancer—those constraints have already been decided—but I might manage to complete this manuscript and get the book published!).

Our choices are constrained by scientific reality and by our previous actions, but the making of meaning transcends scientific knowledge, even as it incorporates that knowledge. It is constrained by the past but not determined by it. The integration of human knowing with human living remains a vital task, conducted in freedom.

For us, then, as for any people seeking to identify with a continuing tradition and to mine the wisdom that tradition preserves, the issue of creation is twofold:

1. Sifting scientific data and theory to arrive at a plausible and likely account of what we can know of the beginning and development of our cosmos

2. Revisiting the sacred stories and literature of our tradition to allow those cultural and spiritual resources to impart the wisdom our new perspectives reveal

That means that creation is for us not merely a scientific imposition—it is also a spiritual and cultural imperative. All people have a stake in this enterprise, and we all need to learn from each other. This book is a guide for us all, explicating the science needed to describe the world accurately, offering the perspective necessary to assemble the facts into meaningful patterns that make human thriving, ethical rigor, and rich spirit possible. Its intended audience sits in concentric circles: Jews who are interested in understanding their heritage in a way that is compatible with science and the best of contemporary values, spiritual seekers of all labels (and none) who want to bring to their journey the fertile structure of Process Thought and the energizing wisdom of Jewish tradition, scientists interested in a thoughtful articulation of how religion can partner in their endeavors, and religious people who seek scientific literacy without having to surrender their faith.

As already noted, this book builds on the edifice established by *God of Becoming and Relationship*, which is a general introduction to Process Theology from a Jewish perspective. This book extends that beyond the introductory level and is intended as the first volume in a trilogy, each focusing on one key cluster of theological value concepts: creation, revelation, and redemption. *Renewing the Process of Creation* will go well beyond the base provided in my previous book, deepening an exploration into how science and religion, each properly understood and honored, can serve the advance of human and planetary thriving.

Unless otherwise specified, biblical and rabbinic verses in English are my own translations. Special attention was paid to maintain gender neutrality in the translations. In that regard, I am happy to acknowledge my debt to the Jewish Publication Society for their translation of the Hebrew Bible.

Allowing new insight to emerge through the voices of the Hebrew Bible and the Talmudic Sages is an age-old Jewish endeavor. Midrash and philosophy have been the ready handmaids for the dynamic feedback among integration, innovation, and harmony that makes possible human wholeness. A future that is honest, unafraid, and authentically continuous (without being slavishly imitative) with its past requires no less a robust commitment.

That commitment is nestled in what I've called the two rooted belongings and entail being human. We are at once a part of all creation, nestled within nature as a whole. And we are conscious of our place in nature and self-conscious at a level that may well be unique. We are called, therefore, to be nature's voice and conscience, to sing its songs and to safeguard its vitality. This book is a summons to that sacred task.

We begin, therefore, with the beginning.

Part I

THE SCIENCES
OF CREATION

Nothing is too wonderful to be true, if it be
consistent with the laws of nature.
—Michael Farraday[1]

We open with an examination of the principal scientific areas that set the
context for what we know of creation—physics and cosmology,
biology and evolution—and then examine how a natural explanation
of the beginning can best account for the universe we actually inhabit.
Our goal in this section will be to present the necessary science to
allow the reader to know the world around us, to recognize our place
in that world, and to be able to hone a sense of marvel and awe that
springs from the world as it actually is.

Science has expanded the picture of our cosmos before our eyes.
We now know that there are billions of galaxies, countless planets
circling their own suns, in skies without end. We know that there are
types of matter unseen, some which might be unseeable and ungov-
erned by any human criteria of reason. We know that the species
currently alive represent only the smallest possible percentage of the
teeming forms of life that once existed, but that somehow all life on
earth is related to all other life. We know that human consciousness
is only one form of mind found on this planet.

Moving continents and a churning core to our planet, myriad forms of life each competing and transforming to take advantage of every possibility earth offers, human mind emerging from our extraordinary brain and nervous system to encompass a shifting and expanding cosmos—these are some of the complex and extraordinary ways that our universe surprises, astonishes, and invites exploration as we consider the many ways that our world is super, natural!

1

Science and Creation
What Are We Seeking?

This divine science [theology] cannot become actual
except after a study of natural science.
—Rabbi Moses Maimonides,
Guide for the Perplexed, introduction[1]

It is clear that physics, chemistry, and biology integrate human perceiving of nature with those natural phenomena observed, that the way people look at information and attempt to gather it is very much shaped by the cultural and scientific expectations they bring to it, and that the expectations in turn are dynamically shaped by what it is they are observing.[2] As we explore the ways that the sciences and Judaism shape an agenda of mutual study and elicit greater information from each other in a sort of dynamic interaction, we are going to be looking at that blend, that mix of ways that what is studied constrains our conclusions, and the ways our expectations and modes of thought constrain what we see.

In that sense it is worth considering the insights of pioneering American scholar Ian Barbour in clarifying the interface of religion and science. Barbour posited that science and religion logically interact in one of four different ways.[3] There are those who see the interaction between the two as an interaction of conflict, so that the claims of biology, the claims of physics, the claims of chemistry on the one hand and the claims of religion on the other are inevitably in conflict with one another. Only one is true and the other must be false. For some forms of religion and for some forms of scientism (the presumption that all of reality is public, testable, and repeatable), that may well be the case. If one believes that revelation and its product—scripture—are the only vehicles for knowing truth and that those vehicles are absolute and literal, then indeed religion and science are on a collision course. The same is true for those for whom science is not merely a mode of inquiry into the public aspects of physical reality but is also coextensive with all of reality, and all of reality is reducible to its most minute parts. So for materialist reductionism (that is, the assumption that all of reality is covered by science, that it is explained exhaustively in terms of its physical components) and for fundamentalist literalists in the religious camp, it may well be that conflict is the only way to understand the relationship between the two disciplines.

Barbour delineated a second group, who incline toward disciplinary independence—those who would hold that religion has its own coherence, its own insights, as does the scientific enterprise, and that the two of them simply do not intersect. So, famously, there are those who argue that science explores how things operate and religion illuminates *why* things operate; for example, evolution explains how the human body developed, but religion determines how we can treat each other's bodies with honor and dignity. In that parallel track, the two disciplines do not really interact at all. If it is a "how" question, such as "How did the human body develop?," it is a science question; if it is "why" question, such as "Why should we treat each other as equal?," it is a religion question. Sometimes religious people use "how" when they really mean "why," as in "How should we meet our obligations to the poor?," which is really asking a why question: what our motives ought to be and why. Nonetheless, the questions and the realms remain distinct. Science is sovereign in its area; religion is sovereign in its area. Religion has very little to contribute to a discussion about the makeup of subatomic reality or of galaxy formation, and science has very little to contribute to conversations about moral goodness, obligation, or awe. The two of them are silent in each other's jurisdiction, restricting themselves within their own sovereignty.

The third mode of interaction, says Barbour, is dialogue, in which the two fields are indeed distinct, separate from each other, but nonetheless engage in a mutually fructifying conversation. Each endeavor benefits from being able to consider the narrative and the laws of the other while remaining two separate practices, not to be blurred, not to be merged; nonetheless, each is refined and enhanced by the encounter with the other. Science can provide information that hones religious questions; for example, knowing that animals do process fear and anxiety, how should we change how we structure zoos or animal use in research armed with this new knowledge? And religion can raise ethical concerns to rule certain experiments unacceptable, just as philosophy can help scientists realize when they are pursuing a scientific agenda and when they are crossing a line to make personal assertions unsupported by the evidence. In this approach, science becomes, in a sense, a corrective to religious superstition, or of a religious slippage toward excessive gullibility, and religion forces science to engage in the living and ethical qualities of the cosmos that it attempts to study.

The fourth and final category that Barbour proposes is what he calls integration. Integration, I think, is where most of us would hope to reside. Integration holds that we live in one single world, a uni-verse, and that one world is somehow susceptible to explanation in a way that aspires, at some point, to be unified. It may well be that we are going to have to take several running steps to be able to get to it; it may well be that for the foreseeable future, we will not be able to express a unified theory that integrates the natural sciences, the social sciences, and the humanities. Perhaps we will have to lean on partial explanations of the world as a whole for quite some time. For example, we can describe how neurons work in the brain and can even highlight active areas linked to particular mental practices in an external third-person perspective, and we continue to experience consciousness from an internal, first-person perspective. We have an intuition that they are somehow connected, but for the present we can't get from the one to the other seamlessly. Nonetheless, many seeking people cherish a conviction that the world masks a oneness to be uncovered,[4] a oneness that somehow encapsulates the very small, the very large, and us in the middle, and that somehow the humanities and the natural and social sciences are all part of a vast but single canvas. From this perspective there ought to be a framework for bringing them into conversation with each other, with the goal of an ultimate unification, a more encompassing realism.

In the exploration of integration, in the attempt to uncover an embracing oneness that encourages the cousins of science and religion each to play productively with each other, and each to become, in a sense, part of each other's story, we seek stability and predictability. But there is also, I believe, a role for serendipity, for chance, for randomness and consciousness. We seek a perspective of the universe in which our intellectual and descriptive understanding includes a place for events that do not have to happen, rather than a universe governed by a mechanistic determinism in which if we know the rules and enough information, we could plot out everything that has to have happened, from the beginning of time to its very end. We perceive ourselves to live in a universe of freedom in which the choices that we and other elements within the world make are able to shape a future that is not dictated, a tomorrow that is somehow profoundly open. How we do that requires thinking about the data of the sciences and the perceptions of human existence. We also seek a role for providence, not necessarily as an outside intrusion from on high, nor as the sense of a future closed to freedom, but nonetheless one in which the Divine is an active and constant partner in the choices that natural agents make, including human agents, and that the Divine somehow permeates or is immediately available in every part of the cosmos, in every manifestation.

And then, finally, most acute of all, many of us seek the possibility of some form of revelation, a way in which, as our ancestors framed it, the Divine is able to erupt into human consciousness, to blossom as words, and those words are able to then nurture the communities and the practices of the people who seek to live in harmony with the Divine distilled into word.

Those three aspects form the framework of this section's inquiry: A role for chance and randomness, which is to say, for freedom; a role for providence, which is to say, for the structures that constrain and shape and make possible the building of systems and individual complexity; and then finally, the possibility of revelation, which is to say, to know the Divine and to be able to live in harmony with the Divine.

Understanding the origins of the cosmos and its implications for the meaning of our lives is no small task. We are both aided and dizzied by the extraordinary advances in cosmology, quantum physics, astrology, biology, and cognitive science. Even as those sciences continue to refine what it is possible to know, they also create new uncertainties, rely on new assumptions, and generate new conflicts within and beyond their own fields. It would be foolhardy to presume to know with certainty when the scientists themselves lack consensus, but our abiding task is to notice when a conversation has reached reliable consensus, when it has transcended the parameters of experimental verifiability to a more (metaphysical) speculation, and to serve as an honest broker in allowing plausible speculation (scientific or philosophical) to generate research agendas within or between disciplines. At the end of it all, our task remains to fashion lives of meaning and integrity, to strengthen communities of love and justice, knowing what we do about the cosmos we inhabit and embody.

2

Cosmology and Physics
A Dynamic, Emerging Universe

Do you know the laws of the heavens or its
authority on earth?
—Job 38:33

Meaning and facts share a mutual influence: it is impossible to determine
what something means without understanding the pertinent facts—
what it is and how it works. It is also impossible to determine which
facts are significant or worthy of exploration without a clear sense
of meaning and values. To understand the import of creation and
our place in the created order, we must turn first to the science of
physics to provide the data for how the universe is composed, how
its entities interact, and how it began.

Earth Marginalized:
Not the Center of the Universe

The first point to note is how recent and swift is the advance of physics. The development of technology in the West made possible the
expansion of our capacity to use empirical methods to explore both
the very large—cosmology, relativity—and the very small—atoms,
subatomic particles, and quantum. As little as a hundred years ago,
most experts "knew" that ours was the only galaxy. As little as five
hundred years ago, the experts "knew" that the earth was at the

center of the entire cosmos. And the origin of the universe, creation, was purely a matter of logical surmises, as there were no facts available to constrain our speculation. We have been able to assess greater amounts of actual data from distant galaxies (photographs of distant early galaxies, light spectra that tell us the composition of the farthest stars, chemical analyses of asteroids and planetary rocks) and the most minute elements of matter (recall recent evidence of the Higgs field, the subatomic relating that gives matter bulk and weight!), previously inaccessible to human experiment or testing, with extraordinary results.

In 1542, the astronomer Copernicus launched this revolution by revealing that it was more useful to think of the sun as the center of our solar system, rather than the earth, followed in the early 1600s by the natural scientist Galileo's findings, with his improvements to the telescope, that the sun itself was imperfect and his speculations that the Milky Way was a collection of sun-like stars. For the first time, this revealed that the same rules that govern matter here on earth also pertain in space, making it possible to make assertions about the nature of distant stars and planets. This startling advance was followed yet again in 1687 by the publication of physicist Isaac Newton's *Principia*, which presented the principles of time, force, and motion in mathematical terms and demonstrated the mechanistic functioning of universal gravity—on earth and throughout the heavens—which conspired to remove any sense of unique centrality to the earth as a location. Newton's insights also made it possible to make predictions and subject the universe to experimental exploration and confirmation. We could know things now that previously we could only surmise! Already by the time of Newton, we had enough information to concede that the earth and humanity were not central in any geographic sense; that the laws pertaining to this planet were no different from the laws that pertain to any other spot in the cosmos. To many people, it felt like a demotion of cosmic proportions!

We forget that at the turn of the twentieth century, most astronomers still believed that the Milky Way was the entire universe, and that it was only in the 1920s that some scientists started to suggest there were galaxies beyond our Milky Way. American astronomer Edwin Hubble resolved this argument in 1924 by charting the distance of the Andromeda Galaxy, the nearest major galaxy to the Milky Way, and a few years later, in measuring the velocity and distance of other astronomical entities, he noted that they were moving away from us at a speed proportional to their distance. What came to be known as Hubble's Law now tells us that space itself is expanding, and it has been used to measure the cosmos to about ten billion light-years, an area with one hundred billion galaxies. The size of the current visible universe is about eighty billion light years. That light has been traveling for about ten billion years, but the cosmos has expanded considerably in that time. By the 1920s, we already knew that the universe is a dynamic, developing, interactive process, vastly larger and more complex than we had previously imagined. We had to rethink what perfection means: the cosmos was no longer static, unchanging, and silent. Everywhere, dynamism, interaction, and relationship ruled supreme.

Common Sense Dethroned: Space and Time Are Not Absolute

Our commonsense perception is that "now" for me is identical with "now" for you—there is an absolute present true for everything. Think about how you call someone local, and it is the same time for them as it is for you. And if you call someone halfway around the globe, you can look up what time it is there with certainty. Our everyday experience of time supports our intuition that time is objective and real. It also seems self-evident that space is an empty container in which matter fits; that intuition works for decorating our homes, planting in our yards, even for throwing a rock off a cliff. All that commonsense insight took a hit in the mid-twentieth century. Whereas Newton's physics assumed that space and time were universal and absolute, Albert Einstein articulated the special theory of relativity, in which he understood space and time to be two manifestations of a single reality, space-time, and he demonstrated the equivalence of mass and energy—the famous formula $E = mc^2$. He also argued that the real absolute of the universe was the speed of light. Theoretical physicist Paul Dirac was able to make particle physics consonant with relativity, predicting in the process the existence of antimatter. As a consequence of these seemingly innocuous assertions, we find ourselves in a universe with time dilation, which is the duration of time between events determined by the velocity and perspective of the participants. There is no absolute present. How do we know this? Well, every time you use your car's GPS, you prove the relativity of time. Those satellites are going fast enough and are high enough that their measurement of time is different from that of those of us driving on the surface of the earth. Our GPS programs automatically have to adjust for that time differential in order to get us to our destinations. NASA's rocket ships and satellites have to take their various velocities and locations into account when they calculate how to land, because mass and length also differ according to the frame of reference of the viewer. Without Einstein's recognition of space-time's relativity, returning satellites would land in the wrong spots or even miss the earth entirely! While Einstein very much holds that the laws of physics are the same everywhere for everyone, what emerges from his construct and has been repeatedly verified experimentally is a space-time continuum in which time, space, mass, and velocity have no uniform absolute measure independent of the viewer's frame of reference. Why does that matter to us? Because the old model was static, objective, solid. The world became a big dead machine, and we were zombies with apparent consciousness, moving in a predetermined lockstep. With the insights of relativity now proven, we know we are living in a universe that is dynamic, that reality is profoundly pluralistic and shaped by relationships between its parts, that our world is profoundly participatory and interactive.

In 1915, Einstein published his account of the general theory of relativity, which incorporated his understanding of gravity not as a force acting on mass, but as a curvature of space-time. As theoretical physicist John Wheeler explains, "Space tells matter how to move, and matter tells space how to curve."[1] Not only space but also time is affected by gravity. Einstein's insights, since empirically verified, radically shifted commonsense perceptions of space, time, gravity, force, and matter in ways that we continue to struggle to integrate into our broader understanding of life itself. Einstein's theories reveal a universe that is dynamic and interconnected:

> Space and time are inseparable, mass is a form of energy, and gravity and acceleration are indistinguishable. There is an interplay between the dynamics of matter and the form of space, a dialectic between temporal process and spatial geometry. Matter is, if you will, a wrinkle in the elastic matrix of spacetime. Instead of separate enduring things, externally related to each other, we have a unified flux of interacting events.[2]

In the 1920s, Russian physicist Alexander Friedmann solved the equations that permitted Belgian cosmologist Georges Lemaitre to realize that space itself was expanding, reasoning backward that the universe began as a point of infinite density some fourteen billion years ago, exploding outward to become the cosmos we now know. The big bang theory, as it came to be known, has received significant support from diverse sources, and contributed to our understanding the variations in the cosmic background radiation (measuring the various temperatures of different places in deep space), its blackbody spectrum (allowing us to know the temperature and composition of distant stars), and the temperature fluctuations that indicate density ripples that made possible the formation of galaxies and clusters of galaxies. More recently, expectations that the universe should be decelerating have been shown to be false; indeed, the evidence suggests that its expansion is accelerating. Many cosmologists now suggest that something called dark energy accounts for this inexplicable and surprising acceleration and are actively seeking ways to verify its existence and its nature.[3] What this means for us is that the world is far from what it appears to be on the surface, that the cosmos is dynamic, nuanced, and endlessly surprising in unpredictable ways.

Tiny and Weird: The Wacky World of Quantum

While physics was advancing in its understanding of the largest-size scales, it was simultaneously making great strides in revealing the quirky and unanticipated world of the very small. Atomic theory in the eighteenth century yielded advances in the field of chemistry and then made a leap when it was discovered that the atom is not solid but is primarily composed of empty space, with nuclei at the center (composed of protons and neutrons) and electrons in orbit around the center. This billiard-ball model gave way, through the insights of quantum theory, to the recognition that these elementary particles are not really particles in any solid, static sense. They are more like probabilities, wave functions, possibilities. Our understanding of the very small is that matter is made up of fundamental events that act more like energy than our sense of solid, stable objects. And we have delineated the four forces that describe matter's interaction—gravity, electromagnetism, the weak force responsible for nuclear decay, and the strong force, which gives the nucleus its stability. Rather than little billiard balls that bang into each other coercively, we now know that the components of reality are interactive, recurrent patterns of energy that impact each other internally and instantly, shaping each other through their dynamic connections. Everything is process.

Quantum theory, associated with the physicists Max Planck, Niels Bohr, and others, pushed our understanding of the component events of reality beyond any previous assumptions.[4] In 1900, Planck demonstrated that energy comes in quanta, discrete units. Seeing energy as particles, yet also as waves, creates two inassimilable models that cannot be merged into a single inclusive image (that is how Bohr used the idea of complementarity). Both describe aspects of reality, and the recourse to one model precludes the simultaneous reference to the other. A group of quantum scientists developed a way of describing atomic and subatomic behavior, but those descriptions further assaulted the common sense of everyday logic: atoms demonstrate a way of changing their state of being over time in a way that is indeterminate; they remain connected across large distances without apparent contact (entanglement). This understanding of atomic and subatomic particles has yielded experimental verification as well as technological success. That means that nature, at its smallest, doesn't follow human logic. Indeed, we know that at its smallest, nature has to be described metaphorically (or mathematically) in mutually incompatible descriptions. And we know that at this level, it is impossible to predict how reality is going to behave. There are statistical probabilities, yes, but we don't live in a deterministic universe. Even at a subatomic level, events are unpredictable and interrelated, and each event seems to act in a way to preserve its own identity as best it can—each element behaves in ways distinct to its unique composition. Each type of particle responds distinctively to the interactions it encounters and engages—there is some degree of self-determination at every level. There is some humble measure of what will emerge into agency, even at the very smallest levels of becoming (manifested, for example, by the Pauli exclusion principle[5]).

However counterintuitive it may be, quantum theory describes a reality that is profoundly relational, dynamic, and interactive. There is, at the quantum level, no such thing as inert, dead matter. Once again, all is Process—relational, dynamic, open, and interactive.

Unpredictable: Chaos, Fractals, and an Open Future

The third broad impulse in contemporary physics with consequences for our Process search for meaning, dynamism, and integration lies with chaos theory. Physicist and philosopher Henri Poincaré first discovered chaos theory in the 1880s. The theory blossomed in the mid-twentieth century in the work of American mathematician and meteorologist Edward Lorenz, who used a computer to simulate weather events. He discovered that his computer's weather predictions differed each time he entered even the same data. Small changes in initial conditions produced large and unpredictable changes in long-term outcomes. Lorenz demonstrated why weather forecasters could not predict the weather beyond a week (which anyone who watches the weather reports already knows!). At the same time, mathematician Benoit Mandelbrot was working with fractals, objects whose irregularity is constant over different scales—patterns in which chaos oscillates into recurrent order that in turn oscillates into a new order of chaos. Currently applied in several fields of science and medicine, chaos theory describes how systems can develop in unpredictable and dynamic ways that appear to be random even when they are statistical or deterministic. Why does this matter?

> Chaos brings a new challenge to the reductionist view that a system can be understood by breaking it down and studying each piece.... For example, even with a complete map of the nervous system of a simple organism ... the organism's behavior cannot be deduced. Similarly, the hope that physics could be complete with an increasingly detailed understanding of fundamental physical forces and constituents is unfounded. The interaction of components on one scale can lead to complex global behavior on a larger scale that in general cannot be deduced from knowledge of the individual components.[6]

The insights provided by chaos theory and fractals supports the Process insight that the future cannot simply be determined by the sum of the past. There is a multitude of possibility that beckons us into an open future that we ourselves determine. Knowing what has already occurred may constrain what is possible, but it doesn't determine it; that is, the initial conditions define and constrain future dynamics, but the outcome is not predictable or replicable, even with the same conditions in place. This remarkable openness has contributed to a sense that reality is not simply the necessary single consequence of previous causes (mechanistic determinism), nor that you can exhaustively describe the world simply by describing its component parts (that's known as reductionism). Built into reality at every level is a multitude of possibilities, a participation in selecting the outcome by the participants themselves, and an unpredictability that makes self-determination real.

A Living Universe: Dynamic, Relational, Unpredictable

Each of these frameworks—relativity, quantum theory, chaos theory—coupled with the careful collection of data, has opened a vision of the cosmos quite different from the one held to be accurate in antiquity, the Middle Ages, or even much of modernity. Far from equating perfection with stasis—the universe, a careful collection of unrelated objects in spheres resting in absolute time and space, with the earth a unique jewel at its geographic center—contemporary physics has restored for us a cosmos that is thoroughly relational, vast beyond the wildest imaginings of our ancestors, in which the constant physical "laws" operative since moments after the big bang continue to operate without exception or interruption, yet continuously generate novelty, complexity, and unpredictability. Matter and energy are different manifestations of an underlying dynamic unity, and the patterns of energy that compose matter act according to their own composition to react uniquely and unpredictably to the rest of the interacting cosmos. Reason remains a vital tool, as does experiment and measurement, but it is reason that must integrate the challenges of quantum behavior at the smallest levels, chaos at larger levels, and cosmos at the largest. The universe is awesome beyond imagination, and reality is complex well beyond what is accessible to our senses.

Contemporary physics elevates a dynamic, relational view of time and temporality, in contrast to the medieval evaluation of timeless stasis as the ideal or the norm. This is the understanding of Process Theology. We now know that an integration of lawfulness and chance manifests at every level of existence, as the regularities themselves allow matter to erupt into unpredictable spontaneity and the chaotic distills into replicable patterns. Contemporary physics also suggests a complex approach that resists a simple material reductionism. As English cosmologist and best-selling author Paul Davies observes:

> Now there is a new paradigm of the creative universe, which recognizes the progressive, innovative character of physical processes. The new paradigm emphasizes the collective, cooperative and organizational aspects of nature; its perspective is synthetic and holistic rather than analytic and reductionist.[7]

Levels of reality emerge that are not explicable by reference to the component parts from which they are constructed (you need multiple molecules of water before wetness emerges, for example; erotic preferences can't be explained on the level of protein interaction; and economic patterns can't be explained by neurology). Recognizing reality as synthetic, dynamic, and cooperative, much of contemporary physics seeks to explain phenomena by the criteria appropriate to the level of the phenomenon being explained, as well as by reference to component parts and their interactions and the larger context of the phenomenon. These insights from physics open us to the wisdom of Process Theology, of a universe that is open, relational, and interactive. We are all participants in a cosmic drama whose next act has not yet been written. Through our choices and our actions, we will help create tomorrow's promise.

3

Biology and Evolution
Everyone's Family!

> How can one despair, seeing that everything evolves
> and ascends? When we penetrate the inner nature of
> evolution, we find divinity illuminated in perfect clarity.
> —Rabbi Abraham Isaac Kook,
> *Orot Ha-Kodesh* 2:537

There was a time when thinkers who attempted to order their thoughts about physics and biology would attempt to distinguish between the two, as though biology was merely a jumble of random information, whereas knowledge of physics was somehow self-evidently the knowledge of an abstract set of laws, which then allowed for the categorizing of physical reality in the context of those laws.[1] Scholars like the seventeenth century's Isaac Newton used mathematics and logic to dope out the regularities by which the universe ought to operate and then in turn used those logical tools to make inquiries successfully about the nature of physical reality. For quite some time, the knowledge of biology was a more complicated collation, organizing life into recognizable patterns (such as phyla and species), with the patterns governing biology harder to discern and a more self-evident role for subjectivity in the identification of those laws. As far back as Aristotle in the fourth century BCE, thinkers attempted to discern patterns within biology, but often one had a sense that those patterns were as much imposed by the thinker as they were extrapolated from the data. The data remained on the level of classification of particulars (such as enumerating different species of beetles) rather than the unveiling of broad universal patterns that constrained the emergent details of living things and their relations, and which in turn complicated deeper understanding. Regardless of whether one attempts to make the grand patterns and the detailed categorization separate, it is clear that in the realm of biology there is a mix of both general narrative and a welter of specific details.

But biology gained coherence and agenda with the advent of evolutionary theory. Since at least the time of Charles Darwin in the nineteenth century, that storyline has gained extraordinary coherence and force by recognizing the overarching narrative provided by evolution, which is a combination of randomness on the part of the larger system (genetic mutation, for example), relationship between the parts and the whole (called natural selection, meaning that some random mutations just happen to provide an advantage for those who carry that shift—like black moths on the soot-covered trees of England's industrial revolution), and responsiveness and intentionality on the part of the participants of the system (think of a lioness choosing one mate over another, chasing one gazelle instead of a second, fleeing this way during a fire rather than a different direction; the next generation—hence, evolution's future—hinges on such decisions). Random change, situational advantage, and deliberate choices—those are the elements that drive evolution forward.

Darwin was able to provide a coherent narrative in which to locate the biological data, which in turn allowed him and his followers to organize greater clusters of information than their predecessors had; the very ability to order the knowledge, to contextualize the knowledge, to relate the knowledge as pieces to a larger puzzle—a coherent puzzle—gave them access to even more information about the biosphere and the world around them.

We live with the heritage of this synergy: biology as narrative together with biology as exemplified in specific details. But the details are not separate from the narrative; they are connected to it and a manifestation of it. In this way, biology—like Judaism—is a complex, dynamic system in which both narrative and detail (practice) form the interacting means by which the living quality of the system operates, by which the dynamism inherent in its participants allows them to connect to each other and to contribute to something greater than any of the individual constituents. The fish in a school or the bees in a hive create something larger than themselves, and the life in a hive or pond also comes together as a unit that is bigger—and different—than its several component individuals. The individuals influence the totality, and the totality in turn impacts the individuals.

The key for organizing the story of biology is the saga of evolution. Articulated simultaneously by British naturalist Alfred Wallace and most famously by Charles Darwin in *On the Origin of Species* published in 1859, augmented by the genetic theory of Gregor Mendel in the 1860s and the DNA breakthrough of James Watson and Francis Crick in 1953, the current theory of evolution, sometimes referred to as Neo-Darwinism, posits and demonstrates three broad assertions: the gradual development of all species from a single origin, the interrelatedness of all living things on earth, and the mechanism of natural selection and random genetic mutation as the driving forces generating speciation and diversity. More recently, diverse voices have drawn attention to the role of deliberate selection—not by some external Designer, but by living creatures, the agents of evolution themselves—and the role of cooperation, collaboration, and mutual support in addition to that of competition in conferring adaptive benefit.

The primary insight of all evolutionary theories is that each life is related to all life. The evidence for this claim begins with genetics and the realization that human beings share between 50 and 99 percent of our genes with other species. Even a relatively small degree of divergence can lead to quite significant distinctions. For example, humans and chimpanzees differ in only 5 percent of their genomes.

The Tree of Life today is a genetic diagram, demonstrating the way that all life shares a common genetic code. All living things, from single-celled organisms through plants and continuing into animal life (including the human), express the same genetic system! That fact alone is an astonishing and powerful demonstration of the unity of all living creatures on earth. That we share more genetically with creatures closer to us on the evolutionary Tree of Life is further evidence of the accuracy and sweep of the evolutionary explanation for life's diversity and commonality. It makes sense that we share more in common with gorillas (with whom we share 96 percent of common genes) than with dogs (82 percent) and more with dogs than with birds (60 percent).

Genes are transmitted from generation to generation, generally with a high degree of stability and reliability. But with each generation's transmission, a small percentage undergoes random mutations—getting the message slightly differently. Generally those mutations are either neutral, neither aiding nor interfering with successful reproduction, or harmful, preventing successful reproduction. In very rare instances, those mutations are advantageous and permit the bearer to produce a greater number of progeny, who in turn are able to produce more progeny (for example, the relatively recent mutation that led to pale skin, blond hair, and blue eyes for people in cold, northern climates, which allowed them to derive maximal benefit from the relatively small amounts of sunlight available to them). This is an example of Charles Darwin's theory of natural selection. Over the course of several generations, accumulated, successive, small changes result in adaptations to the particular environment and the other species living and evolving with that particular species. Notice, for instance, how many species of dog we live with, each one developed by ingenious humans who availed themselves of Darwinian evolution to sculpt the precise look or temperament they wanted in their dog.

In addition to the random selection just considered, it remains true that living things demonstrate deliberate selection (sometimes referred to as artificial selection)—where to live, what to eat, when to sleep, with which individual to mate. That deliberate selection also drives the evolutionary process. Through this mechanism of random mutation, deliberate selection, genetic drift, and fortuitous circumstance, new traits gain traction, eventually leading to sufficient distinctiveness of the offspring that they can no longer reproduce with the original group, leading to the establishment of a new species—in plants, think of the different kinds of roses (or cabbage), and in animals, the famous finches of the Galapagos Island chain reveal this diversity. Through this mechanism, all new species are related to the earlier forms from which they emerged.

That sense of interrelationship is heightened by our renewed appreciation of ecosystems and co-evolution. When we speak of "natural" selection, the nature we mean is an ecosystem—the total context of living and nonliving things with which the individual and the species interact: a pond, a desert, an ocean, a jungle. Each population within an ecosystem occupies its own specific niche, which relates to all other niches in the same ecosystem (and the ecosystem relates to all surrounding ecosystems). This broader vision allows us to recognize that the evolutionary development of a species will be connected to the evolutionary development of every other species in the same ecosystem. This means, among other things, that an adaptation in one species will produce a corresponding adaptation in its prey and its predators (for example, yucca moths and yucca plants). Evolution is a dynamic, in which the constantly shifting characteristics of one species will produce ripples of adaptations in interdependent species, which in turn will stimulate further adaptations in the original species. Bees and specific types of plants have evolved in such a way that they attract each other's attention and their survival requires the partner species—insects and flowers evolving each other. More than evolution, it is preferable to speak of co-evolution, in which every species evolves in sync with every other species in its ecosystem, with the physical as well as biological elements of the local environment. Indeed, this co-evolution manifests within a species as well, for example in the way that we have found cor-related mutations of amino acids within a protein or the integration of mitochondria within eukaryotic cells. Flowers have evolved along with birds' bills so that particular birds can feed on particular flow-ers, thereby ensuring their successful pollination. There is no solitary evolving; each process is connected not only to the inherited genes of all preceding life but also to the choices, challenges, and opportu-nities of all other members of the same region.

Not all of this co-evolution involves conflict. There are many recorded cases of mutually beneficial adaptations, between plants and fungi, among different animals, even between organisms of the same species. Colonies of insects, somatic cells within an animal's body, kin assistance and support—each of these examples high-lights ways that cooperation exerts an important co-evolutionary survival benefit. Evolution is not the external interaction of solitary individuals nor even of species in isolation. Like the evidence from more recent physics, contemporary biology draws our attention to the dynamic embeddedness of each species with every other inter-acting species, of each individual with every other individual of the same group and of interacting groups. In short, biology, like physics, reveals a world of relationships and dynamic interaction, rather than separate selves bumping into timeless forms. If what it means to be a zebra shifts, then simultaneously what it means to be a lion no lon-ger remains the same. Living, like all other phenomena, is dynamic, relational, and interactive. And, like simpler matter, each event (or creature) manifests its own appropriate agency. Plants grow toward this direction and not that, and there are consequences to their "choice." Amphibians enter this pond and not that one, birds mate with this partner and not that one, bison wander from this plain to that one. Their choices in turn impact upon the co-evolution of their own species, of the species that interact with their own, and on the ecosystems within which they struggle, cooperate, and advance.

Some have argued—most notably paleontologist Stephen Jay Gould and geneticist Richard Lewontin—that the very things we look to as making life rich and worthwhile—such as consciousness, emotions, joy, Eros—are epiphenomenal, what they call "spandrels." Spandrels were the unintended consequence in medieval architecture of creating domes over cubed rooms, which resulted in triangular spaces between the flat lintel and the arched dome that no one had intended, but which cried out for additional decoration. To say that the church had been built for the sake of the spandrel would be incorrect. The spandrel was simply the fortuitous product of a certain type of architecture that created an additional and unanticipated space. Once the space was present, the artisans used it for other purposes; the spandrels were not deliberately created to make space for more art. Gould and others have argued that many of those areas of life to which we point as looking like what evolution created are, in fact, the spandrels of evolution (some have pointed to the development of language or music as spandrels emerging from the evolution of the human brain). They were not intended for the particular purpose for which they were subsequently drafted. They were not what was pushing the evolutionary change. They were simply an unanticipated epiphenomenon of the push to survive:

> Evolutionary biology needs such an explicit term for features arising as byproducts, rather than adaptations, whatever their subsequent exaptive utility.... Causes of historical origin must always be separated from current utilities; their conflation has seriously hampered the evolutionary analysis of form in the history of life.[2]

That characterization may well be explanatory from one perspective, but it is nonetheless also evident that in addition to natural selection and heritable mutation, evolution is driven by the relentless and constant choosing that the participants in evolution make themselves. Natural selection, after all, is somebody making a choice that has survival consequences: the selection of *this* spouse as opposed to that one, *this* mate as opposed to this one, *these* offspring as opposed to no offspring, *this* food as opposed to that food, *that* activity as opposed to this activity, mobilizing to take a risk or choosing to play it safe by laying low. Living entities seek to advance their own continuous teleology, but this teleology bubbles up from within rather than being imposed from above or from without. "The stone that the builders rejected has become the chief cornerstone" (Psalm 118:22): it may well be that it was the very spandrel that some creature found alluring—in a mate, in a meal, in a locale. That spandrel was given a significance in subsequent evolution that supplemented and transcended mere fortuity. In a deeper sense, everything in evolution is a spandrel, and nothing is.

As with physics, the rich harvest of biology offers us a vision that is profoundly interactive and relational. The cosmos and its denizens are co-evolving and inter-dynamic in that the character of objects, creatures, and groups are engaged in processes of change and coherence generated by taking in the data of the dynamic cosmos and responding to those changes according to each event's previous choices, nature, and possibilities. Chance and intention, constraints and choice, established character (and characteristics), generating novel responses—these dipolarities offer an ever-shifting integration of continuity and change, of coherence and innovation. "Creation" is our term for this shifting, unending process of growth, diversification, coordination, and co-evolution. Every day, constantly, the cosmos and its creations, the world and its creatures are renewed and are self-renewing. Centers of agency, the creatures participate in and contribute to the processes that are creation. Self-evolving, creation continues to renew itself. Biology is best understood in the context of Process Thought, because life is a continuous series of events: a process of processes.

This ongoing integration of stability and dynamism, of constraints and possibilities has generated novelty for billions of years. This unlikely eruption of unprecedented events, of creatures who have never before existed, of ever more complex capacities for experience and mindfulness calls for explanation: Do these new occasions, erected out of the building blocks of processes that are more fundamental, actually explain reality themselves, or are they fully accounted for when we've delineated their basic building blocks? If they aren't composed of anything new, in what sense do they exist at all? In other words, if a fish is simply composed of physical elements and chemical compositions, is a fish anything beyond what it's made of? What additional do we mean by "fish"?

We turn our attention, therefore, to the emergence of complexity and of the living processes that make our world worth experiencing in the first place.

4

Emergence, Fine-Tuning, and the Anthropic Principle

An Unlikely World That Fits Us Perfectly!

> Behold, everything is bound together in one thing....
> Now, let everything emerge and be perfectly arranged.
> —*Zohar* 3:65a

Evolutionary concepts not only pertain to the processes of biology, but also extend backward conceptually to help clarify and explicate the cosmic becomings that precede the biosphere. Through a feedback among natural selection, chance, and the particular nature of the specific elements or conglomerations of elements and their efforts toward homeostasis against great pressure and odds, the cosmos self-diversified into the astonishing array of galaxies, star systems, and space (and if we live in a multiverse, then the evolution of this particular space-time bubble may itself reflect Darwinian dynamics).[1] One of those galaxies developed our blessed, stable solar system, which generated a geosphere capable of transmuting into first water, then simple life, then oxygen, then complex life, and finally emerging into consciousness. In a continuous cascade of evolutionary development, an intricate interplay of coercion and freedom, of natural efforts to preserve dynamic equilibrium and equally natural efforts to disrupt equilibrium, the universe evolved into the complex interactive processes it is today:

> The universe is neither a random gas nor a crystal, but a menagerie of coherent, organized, and interacting systems forming a hierarchy of structure. Nature is thus a potent mix of two opposing tendencies, in which there is pervasive spontaneity and novelty, providing openness in the way the universe evolves but enough restraint to impose order on the products. The laws of nature thus bestow on the universe a powerful inherent creativity.[2]

This unlikely emergence of nature's complexity and diversity is made possible by a remarkable specificity of physical "laws," patterns embodying natural processes that allow not only for chance but also for the emergence of genuine novelty and complexity. These particular physical constraints reflect a fine-tuning that is so statistically improbable as to beckon beyond randomness, toward intentionality:

- The cosmos is so vast because there is one crucially important huge number N in nature, equal to 1,000,000,000,000,000,000,000, 000,000,000,000,000. This number measures the strength of the electrical forces that hold atoms together, divided by the force of gravity between them. If N had a few less zeros, only a short-lived miniature universe could exist: no creatures could grow larger than insects, and there would be no time for biological evolution.

- Another number, E, whose value is 0.007, defines how firmly atomic nuclei bind together and how all the atoms on earth were made. Its value controls the power of the sun and, more sensitively, how stars transmute hydrogen into all the atoms of the periodic table. Carbon and oxygen are common, whereas gold and uranium are rare, because of what happens in the stars. If E were 0.006 or 0.008, we could not exist.

- The cosmic number Ω (omega) measures the amount of material in our universe—galaxies, diffuse gas, and dark matter. Ω tells us the relative importance of gravity and expansion energy in the universe. If this ratio were too high relative to the particular critical value, the universe would have collapsed long ago; had it been too low, no galaxies or stars would have formed. The initial expansion speed seems to precisely fall into that narrow range in which a stable growing universe is possible.

- Measuring the fourth number, λ (lambda), was the biggest scientific news of 1998. An unsuspected new force—a cosmic antigravity—controls the expansion of our universe, even though it has no discernible effect on scales less than a billion light-years. It is destined to become ever more dominant over gravity and other forces as our universe becomes ever darker and emptier. Fortunately for us—and very surprisingly to theorists—λ is very small. Otherwise, its effect would have stopped galaxies and stars from forming, and cosmic evolution would have been stifled before it could even begin.

- The seeds for all cosmic structures—stars, galaxies, and clusters of galaxies—were all imprinted in the big bang. The fabric of our universe depends on one number, Q, which represents the ratio of two fundamental energies and is about 1/100,000 in value. If Q were even smaller, the universe would be inert and structureless; if Q were much larger, it would be a violent place in which no stars or solar systems could survive, dominated by vast black holes.

- The sixth crucial number has been known for centuries, although it is now viewed in a new perspective. D is the number of spatial dimensions in our world, and equals three. Life could not exist if D were two or four. Time is a fourth dimension but distinctively different from the others in that it has a built-in arrow: we "move" only toward the future. Near black holes, space is so warped that light moves in circles, and time can stand still. Furthermore, close to the time of the big bang, and also on microscopic scales, some speculate that space may reveal its deepest underlying structure of all: the vibrations and harmonies of objects called "superstrings," in a ten-dimensional arena.[3]

Had any of these numbers been slightly different, there would have been no stability, no creativity, no life, and no consciousness. There is surely something riveting about the extraordinary calibration and interaction of these basic forces.[4] Many authors have noted the anthropic coincidences of the physics of the cosmos—the remarkable way that it is susceptible to the human mind, the beauty and harmony of nature, even the remarkable precision of how the forces of nature appear tweaked to make the eventual evolution of life and consciousness possible and even likely.[5] As Canadian philosopher John A. Leslie notes:

> Physicists and cosmologists have been accumulating much evidence that the observed universe is "fine tuned for producing life" in the following technical sense: tiny changes in its general properties would have made it a universe in which no life-forms could appear.[6]

For many Process thinkers—and others—today, the extraordinary precision of these numbers, the narrowness of their possible range to produce sufficient stability for matter and the emergence of life and consciousness, suggests the location of divinity not in the gaps of scientific knowledge but in the very grounding of these calibrations. No longer a *deus ex machina* descending when our factual knowledge breaks (temporarily), this line of thought sees divinity in the constraints and possibilities uniquely calibrated to make stability, and then life, possible. This new teleological argument is called the strong anthropic argument,[7] but the name is misleading because it does not in any way imply that humans are the necessary outcome or the capstone of the cosmic process. This theory is not about human supremacy, inevitability, or necessity. It considers the amazing long shot that each of these numbers reflects, and how even more far-fetched is their interrelatedness, and it deduces that the cosmos looks a lot like it was coordinated and predisposed toward complexity, life, and consciousness. The specific path that life and consciousness manifested is fortuitous; that something would emerge into consciousness seems like a setup. Divinity, in this understanding, is pervasive and constantly luring creation to blossom into emergent complexity, diverse life-forms, one (or several) of which could emerge into awareness and self-consciousness. That the cosmos is so calibrated to produce consciousness and that it is intelligible and yields reliable information and patterns that correspond to mathematics, a symbol system generated within human thought, strike many as so unlikely as to invite an embrace of cosmic intentionality, intelligibility, and unity.[8] We glean intimations of mind and cosmos as expressive of a oneness that pervades all and becomes manifest through all, as we contemplate the cosmos of which our consciousness is an expression and from which it emerges. Out of the One, many; through the many, One.

Marvelous Emergence of New Complexities

The paradox is that the universe began as something quite simple, yet has become increasingly complex and dynamic since its inception. While the evolutionary story is one of monist uniformitarianism—an insistence that the patterns pertaining today pertained from the very beginning without a break, applying not only here but in every part of this space-time bubble—it is still clear that the cosmos today is significantly more complex than it was at its initial explosion into/ as space-time. These fundamental patterns are essential to any understanding, but they do not describe or predict all there is to know, precisely because what emerges as a result of these very propensities is genuinely novel, because these specific patterns create real openness in the universe as each new level must be explained in terms of its own level (chemistry in terms of chemistry; biology in terms of biology; culture in terms of culture). Each unprecedented advance has an impact on the subsequent nature of reality, and that impact is real, unpredictable in advance, and consequential in turn. The theory that seeks to honor the novelty of new creations and the reality of their impact, yet locates that unfolding within the constraints of physical and natural law and a continuous evolutionary process, is called emergence.

Emergence theory recognizes that the whole is often more than the sum of its parts (think of how unpredictable water is if all you have to consider are separate hydrogen and oxygen atoms

or a Michelangelo statue if all you have are quarries of marble).
Emergence theory reminds us that there are real phenomena—
measured by existence, impact, agency, and causality—that cannot
be described, predicted, or accounted for purely by a description of
their components (any rodent or bird is far more than the sum total
of its anatomy—skeleton, muscle, blood, and so on). From quantum particles and strings to atoms to molecules to cells to organisms
to nonhuman animals to humans, to consciousness and spirit, to
society and culture, genuinely new emergents require explanation at
their own level, or else they are merely explained away (try explaining social structure in terms of genetics or a poem in terms of biochemistry and you'll see what I mean; new complexities emerge that
can only be understood on their own terms). At each new level of
complexity, unanticipated novelties emerge that cannot be reduced
to the qualities of their components. For example, you can't understand "wetness" at a subatomic level; you need large collections of
water molecules before wetness manifests. And you can't understand
love in terms of individual neurons; you need an entire brain inside
a living mammal before you see what love can do.

Emergence seeks a middle path (a *derekh ha-beinoni*) between the
material reductionists, who assert that everything can—in theory, at
least—be completely explained by recourse to its fundamental components, and the dualists, who assert that there are two irreducible
substances—physical and spiritual/mental—that interact somehow
and together account for all things and every activity. Physical objects,
according to a dualist understanding, occupy space and time and can
be explained by physical laws, but mental (or spiritual) entities—
minds and souls—do not occupy space and time and cannot be ana-
lyzed or understood materially. Emergence is an effort to conserve
the oneness of all existence as emerging out of physical, chemical,
biochemical, biological, cultural substrates, but at the same time
honoring the novelty and irreducibility of what emerges at each new
level of complexity.

Reductionism—explaining something by accounting for its components and their interactions—is at the heart of scientific method and has been remarkably productive as a technique, both in expanding our understanding and in producing extraordinary advances in technology and medicine. With reductionism as an epistemological method—an essential tool for knowing—I have no quarrel; indeed I insist on its necessity and centrality for ongoing scientific research and the fullest possible understanding of reality. But many scientists go well beyond reductionism as a methodological assumption and identify themselves as strong reductionists, insisting that there is no thing, no pattern, no behavior that will not yield to a full explanation through the final components of matter and the rules that govern them. This *ontological* reductionism insists that the whole really is nothing but its parts. Emergence seeks to refute that ontological reductionism.

Much is at stake here. For ontological reductionists, the only ultimate reality is that of subatomic particles—or strings, perhaps. Explain what these are and how they interact and then, in theory, one has explained everything; everything else is nothing but a reorganization of an underlying reality, not reality itself (noted physicist and popular author Paul Davies and others have labeled this insistence on "nothing but ..." as "nothing buttery"). "Nothing but ..." means that such value concepts[9] as consciousness, ethics, community, love, loyalty, even life are really epiphenomena and are ultimately illusory. Clearly religion, a sense of holiness, and duty also evaporate as merely apparent but not real. Such reductionism fails to explain most of human perception or motivation, including the urge for scientific research itself. More importantly, such reductionism isn't demonstrated or proved by data; it is a metaphysical assumption into which the facts are crammed.

Emergence, to the contrary, insists that new orders of complexity emerge from earlier orders and that each new emergent order has its own reality as well as its own tools for comprehension and explanation appropriate for that level. Physics can best explain physics (if you want to explain what "hot" really is, then atomic motion and energy are your best bet), but it holds no privilege to reduce away chemical entities or processes, which require the tools, logic, and interactions unique to chemistry. Chemistry, in turn, establishes the constraints for biology but cannot adequately explain biological phenomena. For that explanation, the biologist brings the tools, ideas, and methods of biology. Human mindfulness emerges from the constraints of biology and must be explained using the tools of neuroscience, psychology, and anthropology. Each new emergent level is embedded in the previous level, constrained by that earlier level, but not explicable in terms of the categories, components, or relationships of the embedding level. In such a view, then, community becomes an emergent reality, as does consciousness, religion, or ethics—not reducible to the levels in which they are embedded, and requiring their own levels of understanding. Each is no less real than the levels from which it emerges.

These emerging patterns of complexity do not supplant or contradict the generalizations and systems from which they emerge. Chemistry does not contradict physics, but it does build beyond it. Biology does not repeal the constraints of chemistry, but it goes beyond them. Emergence recognizes the supplemental relationship of nature's different levels of complexity and of the relativist perception that each is real from its own vantage point. Emergence not only recognizes the extraordinary balance of these systems and their practices but also notes that the products of these generalizations become contributing factors in nature's subsequent development. Reality is not simply the mechanical sum total of its component parts, but an evolving, interacting, and self-surpassing process. As physicist Paul Davies notes, this view "depends on a much more fecund understanding of nature than the one usually given by scientists."[10] Expressed plainly, the fundamental constraints of physics and quantum mechanics and the bare mechanisms of the Neo-Darwinian synthesis do not explain the full range of natural creativity, do not by themselves account for how the cosmos went from a very simple state to the extraordinary complexity we see today. For the fullest understanding, we must encounter each emergent layer of reality on its own terms, integrating the emergence of that layer from its preceding layers but also explicating the fruitful fullness of its own dynamism and components.

As philosopher Philip Clayton has pointed out more than once,[11] emergence asks us to understand "reality" in terms of causality: if an agent has causality, then that agent is irreducibly real. There is no other measure of reality that does not presuppose the very outcome in question. But if causality is the fittest measurement of reality, then surely it is clear that cause works in both directions: the simple and component parts can influence the complex and the totality, but the complex also have a feedback impact on the simple and the component. Genes and natural selection do shape evolution, but the choices made by humanity as a whole also activate certain genes and modify the parameters of selection in turn. Higher emergents do have a causal impact on previous levels from which they emerge and are therefore real. To select just a few examples, the behavior of molecules has an impact on the atoms of which they are composed, the behavior of living cells affects the molecular components of the cell, the behavior of multicellular plants and animals modifies the cellular components of which they are made, mental choices have biological—and indeed environmental—consequences. For instance, choosing to eat well and exercise changes the behavior of our genes in maintaining our bodies. How we love our children will prune their brain's neurons to constrain their characteristics for the rest of their lives. These causal impacts are not predictable based solely on knowledge of the behavior or interactions of the component parts, nor are they predetermined. The ways that "higher" levels, like minds, impact "lower" levels, like protein or neuron formation (or, if you prefer a different image, the ways that "wholes" impact "parts"), manifest and generate freedom, complexity, and novelty.[12] Any discussion of what is real cannot begin by defining away a significant aspect of reality, our perceptions and consciousness—the very tools that have made possible scientific inquiry and advance. If we accept the harvest of science as real, must we not then also accept as real the processes that make science happen? We perceive ourselves to be free, to be agents, to act and to cause. That crucial aspect of reality affirms a perspective that is holistic, relational, and creative as better able to account for all of reality than the alternative explanation of reductionism and the world as a big dead machine.

The metaphysical view that articulates this uniformitarian evolutionary emergentist monism transcends the outmoded dichotomy that God's actions are either interventionist—from outside of nature, as most dominant/Orthodox theologies insist—or non-interventionist, as some liberal theologians and Deists would hold. Instead, this Process view of an evolutionary cosmos, one that self-creates into greater novelty and creativity, understands God in dipolar fashion, as both beyond *and* pervading creation, as organizing *and* selecting the parameters and the characteristics of becoming that make such outcomes possible. God fashions, manifests, and invites a sufficiently extravagant cosmos—the infinite quantum fluctuation, the big bang—with just the right characteristics for such relationships and dynamism to emerge, making possible a self-organizing and self-complexifying cosmos that can blossom into consciousness.

Faced with a cosmos that began in the big bang, we confront an astonishing fortuity and fine-tuning about the initial constraints out of which our natural patterns emerged, making possible stability and novelty, life and mind. In the realm of physics and chemistry, as well as in the realm of biology and consciousness, we have seen the old view of mechanical forces that impact objects externally give way to a new view that is holistic, relational, emergent, and creative. Before proceeding with the theological implications of this re-centering, we need to nuance another stubborn remnant from the dominant worldview—the eternity and objectivity of natural "law."

5

A Copernican Proposal
Natural Events and Their Emergent Patterns

It is the natural course of the world.
—Talmud, *Avodah Zarah* 8a

I think it fair to say that most people today view the laws of nature the way many dominant theologians view God—as objective, eternal, and unchanging. They hold these laws to exist in some pure abstraction, above and beyond the particular manifestations in the concrete realm of matter and energy. Physical things conform to these timeless laws, which determine their behavior and shape their future. Gravity makes things fall. Matter can't be created or destroyed. The laws of thermodynamics dictate that disorder increases inexorably.

Eternal Laws, Predetermined Future

This echo of Platonic Forms continues to shape the ideologies, vocabulary, and metaphysics of many of today's educated citizens, scientists, and philosophers. This unexamined presumption can lead to determinism, the conviction that with enough data we can specify all outcomes in advance, and to reductionism, the belief that explaining the components explains the totality. It can also lead to a dichotomy between law and nature. Its classic expression is found in the musings of late eighteenth-century French scholar Pierre Simon, Marquis de LaPlace, whose thought experiment posited a demon in a closed Newtonian world. He noted that in such a mechanistic system, once the initial conditions were known and specified, all subsequent states would be fixed and known as well:

> We ought then to regard the present state of the universe as the effect of its anterior state and as the cause of the one which is to follow. Given for one instant an intelligence which could comprehend all the forces by which nature is animated and the respective situation of the beings who compose it—an intelligence sufficiently vast to submit these data to analysis—it would embrace in the same formula the movements of the greatest bodies of the universe and those of the lightest atom; for it, nothing would be uncertain and the future, as the past, would be present to its eyes.[1]

LaPlace shared today's widespread assumptions that eternal laws, coupled with complete initial data, specify all data for all time. Much of today's science assumes a one-on-one correspondence between idealized mathematical operations and natural phenomena, in which the evolution of physical reality is forever determined by differential equations that exist objectively and timelessly. Like the Neo-Platonists' God, immutable mathematical formulae and relationships are transcendent and ontologically supreme. The laws are absolute and infinitely precise. They determine all particular states of nature but are themselves prior to, independent of, and unconstrained by nature. The laws are beyond space-time—although they determine space-time—and the laws create and shape creation from the moment of the big bang until the present, themselves without change. Furthermore, the laws are posited to be a unity, however much that unity continues to evade theoretical expression and experimental verification.[2] Eternal law precedes ephemeral creation, ontologically and chronologically.

Eternal, static, objective law (somehow) creates and determines contingent physical reality. (This leap across categories exposes the same weak link in the metaphysics of physics as it does in theology.) Reality evolves according to the limits and guidelines of these eternally existing, static laws, and those same laws predetermine nature's future. While the laws determine nature, natural phenomena do not modify the laws. Such a view reflects the theological roots of physics in a dominant theology of a timeless, objective, supernatural Spirit whose eternal law shapes and constrains all material creation, echoing the same spirit/material dichotomy we examined and rejected in the introduction.[3] Indeed, it remains its contemporary expression.

Not Laws, Patterns: The Priority of Actual Events

Without rejecting the evocative utility—indeed, the majesty—of this metaphoric portrayal of physical laws, might we not profit here by making explicit its metaphoric nature? Embracing this dualistic perspective as if it were literal and objective perpetuates several defects: predeterminism (no real creativity is possible), reductionism (no emergent complexity is real), and a constricted view of what counts as significant. Recontextualizing this understanding as the metaphor system it is, we are then free to supplement it with other, more dynamic ways of framing the relationship between generalized patterns, which in turn have predictive utility, and specific phenomena, which generate those patterns and also instantiate them.[4]

Instead of positing an ideal—and experimentally impossible—priority of timeless law that then generates and constrains natural material phenomena, let us assert what we can indeed know: the priority of actual events in nature. Matter is energy frozen; energy is heated matter. I shall refer to both matter and energy as natural events or processes. We can know these events empirically. Each natural event manifests certain physical constraints, which we know in the measurement or experience of the particular events. As we measure or experience groups or series of natural events, we are able to generalize patterns of behavior or characteristics from the specific details of the events' individual processes. These generalizations are refined through further measurement and through their predictive utility, but they, the "laws," remain secondary and approximate.[5] They are derived from real events. Only the events themselves are actual and concrete. The "laws" are composite measurements of multiple concrete events, expressed as mathematical formulae, generalizations that provide superb tools for compiling and understanding, which generate further research projects in turn.[6]

This reconceptualization of the primacy of natural events that act in patterns, which we label "laws" as shorthand, rejects a Platonic conceptualization of a dualistic reality.[7] No surprise, then, that the biblical and rabbinic authorities share our perception: in speaking of the biblical/rabbinic views of miracles, contemporary theologian and founder of European Masorti Judaism, Rabbi Louis Jacobs, notes that miracles do not involve a suspension "of natural or universal law (of which there was no such conception in their thinking)."[8] The Hebrew Bible doesn't have a concept of natural law, neither in the realm of physics nor in that of ethics. Nor do the ancient Rabbis. They are aware that nature often acts in familiar ways ("the world follows its natural course"; Talmud, *Avodah Zarah* 54b), but the Rabbis insist that there are no eternal laws that fix nature's behavior for all time. With this recalibration, the strict dichotomy between law and nature dissolves—law is the extrapolated generalization of patterns demonstrated by recurrent natural events. Events are actual; the generalizations are abstractions one step removed from experience.

Renowned physicists John Wheeler, Rolf Landauer, Paul Davies, and Gregory Chaitin are some of the voices that provide the tools for this Copernican recalibration. Wheeler[9] and Landauer[10] suggest that the most useful image for conceiving of how matter and patterns relate is to think of information as the beginning of the explanatory narrative of physical reality. Information—what Wheeler calls "bits"—is the core data that events, meaning matter and energy, are able to preserve and transmit. "Laws" emerge from the properties of events, and our perception of these patterns reflects the intersubjective, embodied metaphoric way we conceptualize natural events, explore, describe, organize, and predict them. There is no such "thing" as gravity; it is the name we give to recurrent examples of how matter bends space. So gravity is a useful metaphor of relationship, but it does not exist separate from the interactions it describes. Our "laws" are neither objective and eternal nor subjective and cultural.

Instead, this third way, of biologically processing the nature of which we are a part—in which we are embedded and for which we articulate the consciousness—is the human way of discovering reliable patterns in the behavior and characteristics of natural events. This Process approach allows us to recognize that natural events are primary, that what we describe as natural law reflects the patterns and characteristics that natural events manifest individually and in groups. There is thus no ontological gap between laws and events. We are able to recognize that as natural events evolve and develop, the laws can and should develop as well—just as there is no absolute time or space. We can see that the laws co-evolve along with the phenomena that generate them. All is dynamic, relational, interconnected, and self-determining. As natural events, including humanity, continue to self-create and to interrelate, they emerge into novel expressions and developing patterns, at once connected to what came before but able to transcend those constraints. The unity we embody and seek is no longer the mystery of transcending dualism but emerges organically from the dynamic interaction of matter and energy at every moment of evolution, at every level of becoming. There was never any time when natural events were in isolation from each other; there was never any place in which natural events were separated completely. Oneness is itself the expression of emergent, dynamic monism—contemplated and expressed through embodied metaphor.[11]

Viewing the cosmos through these old/new lenses—of dynamic relationship, of the priority of actual events whose behavior can be usefully abstracted as "law," of a universe growing toward greater complexity, experience, and awareness—we are now prepared to perceive the miraculous creation in which we live, breathe, and have our being. We are now ready to become that creation's voice.

Part II

CREATION THEOLOGY IN THE LIGHT OF SCIENCE

Loving God's creatures is closeness to the Blessing One.
—Rabbi Simcha Zissel Ziv, *Sefer Hokhmah*
U-Mussar 1:30

Girded and informed with a scientifically defensible view of nature as dynamic, relational, and open, we are now in a position to ask ourselves: what can it possibly mean for us? In this section, we will apply what we've learned about physics and cosmology, biology and evolution, and psychology and cognitive science to locate our place in the cosmos. We seek to know how to best connect to the rest of teeming, becoming, evolving nature. At the same time, we also desire to know what we are to do: how do we mobilize our focus and actions to maximize justice, love, and dignity?

We consider the lure toward freedom. In this section, I deal with freedom as a metaphysical and physical capacity to make choices that reflect autonomous choice and are not merely the necessary consequence of previous causes. Political freedom, or individual liberty, will concern us in later chapters and subsequent volumes.

This section opens, then, by reflecting on what it means to live in a dynamic universe, in which we are related to all and connected to all. In the light of that awareness, we will retell the story of all being, this time with ourselves within the narrative, the singing voice of the cosmos. We will look to perceive the Divine permeating all becoming and inviting us and all creation forward, each locus of activity equipped with the consciousness and self-determination appropriate to its nature.

A cosmos that is open and dynamic is also one that advances freedom as its mode of becoming. We and all creation help shape the future that actualizes from among the possible futures. We will give focused attention to the nature of the freedom, understood as self-determination, choice, and appropriate agency for all aspects of creation.

Finally, we will celebrate the dynamism and freedom to which we are all called with a cosmic *dayenu*, "it is sufficient!"

6

Dynamic Universe
Self-Determining at Every Level

All the stars and spheres possess a soul,
knowledge, and intellect. They are alive and stand
in recognition of the One who spoke and
thus brought the world into being.
—Rabbi Moses Maimonides, *Mishneh Torah,*
Yesodei Ha-Torah 3:9

Rav Saadia Gaon (ninth-century Baghdad) notes, "There is no means of proving the existence of a Creator other than that of creation."[1] As have others before and after him, he sought to discern the Creator by reading creation. At least since the philosophy of Immanuel Kant in the eighteenth century, the pursuit of natural theology has become problematic, if not impossible. When Kant demonstrated that we are able to know only how the mind organizes reality but not reality as it is independently, he imposed an ironclad dichotomy intended to sunder forever the simple link between the works of creation and the Creator. Even reconceived as embodied metaphor, Kant's insight stands as a warning against equating those attributes of nature a theologian might select to a divine source; the possibility for abuse and distortion remains abiding and real.

Nonetheless, if we are no longer constrained by a rigid fact/ value dichotomy, and if we understand mind as a process of the universe itself emerging into consciousness, if we recognize the "laws" to be the patterns of natural events, then we no longer have to describe God as radically separate from creation and outside space-time. Instead, we are looking for traces of divine relating—through novelty, experience, ethics—that permeate creation and become active through our fellow creations and in us. In that light, the words of Rav Saadia ring true in a new context: we seek to understand the process that is divine through understanding better the implications of the process that is creation.

Cascading Life: We Are One and Ever-Changing

Just as facts are already value-laden and values are already steeped in facts, so our consideration of scientific data has articulated values and perspectives to which we can now give more explicit theological consideration. The first of these fact/values is that of evolution and creation, a battle between those who would insist that every detail of material reality was foretold and established in advance and those who see real openness in the process of creation. The battle lines are surprising and the alliances unexpected. For religious fundamentalists, nothing happens in the world without God's prior intention, so real innovation and agency are precluded. For scientific reductionists on the physics side, nothing happens that is not the simple application of each phenomenon's component physics constrained by eternal law, so real innovation and agency are ruled out. On the other hand, scientific reductionists on the biology side would insist that everything is random, unpredictable, and the expression of an evolutionary process, so that there is randomness without purpose.

Our third way beckons between these chastening straits: a cosmos characterized by dynamism, relationship, and openness; a universe in the process of becoming, an open future awaiting the actions chosen by our free agency.

The first and, I think, most profound, reality of an evolving, emergent, dynamic creation is that every natural event is related to every other natural event and to all natural events. As Process philosopher Alfred North Whitehead points out, "God is not to be treated as an exception to all metaphysical principles, invoked to save their collapse. He is their chief exemplification."[2] Creation theology begins with the insight that it is not God alone who is one. All is a unity. We are related to each and to all, as is the Creator.

That all is one is both fact and value. The big bang produced hydrogen and helium, but it was the first generations of supernovae that exploded the other elements into the dark skies, flinging the nitrogen, carbon, and other essentials for building life into the cosmos. Enough of these elements were collected by the swirling dust that became the solar system and the earth, and the earth was just the right distance from the sun, stabilized by its oversized moon, that it was able to maintain sufficient stability for the emergence of an oxygen-dominated atmosphere, for the emergence of water, for a sufficiently narrow temperature range that the water didn't freeze or evaporate, that organic chemicals could bond, could self-organize in increasingly complex and self-replicating patterns, that single-celled life could commence. That simple life partnered with other single cells (the current theory for the existence of mitochondria and nuclei within cells), and those cells could band together cooperatively to create more complex creatures. Cascading out of this fountain of life (*makor chayim, fons vitae*), some of these new life-forms emerged and greened our earth, rooting themselves in sea rock, sand, and eventually risking the dirt. Their children spread as lichen, shrub, and tree, proliferating as the great forests and jungles that cradled the earth, rooting into the very earth they transformed by their presence and stretching toward the light, "mount and hill shall shout aloud, and all the trees of the field shall clap their hands. Instead of the brier, a cypress shall rise; instead of the nettle, a myrtle shall rise. These shall stand as a testimony to the Holy One, as an everlasting sign that shall not perish" (Isaiah 55:12).

Others of these new children emerged as the soft simple creatures of the sea, some as the myriad bacteria and the swarming insects whose buzzing communities still sustain and pollinate for us all—their distant cousins' progeny. Some of their children's children morphed into the backboned fish, some of their riskier offspring leaped into the swamps and ponds of amphibian aspiration. A few of these frogs and newts boldly dared into drier parts, and their reptile offspring sprouted sturdy legs for walking the land or erupted in plumaged wings to soar on high. Some of their children's children became mighty ponderous dinosaurs, and some others became the tiny warm mammals that scurried underfoot until the dinosaurs' demise shoved the timid furry ones onto a path of diversification and growth that produced woolly mammoths, saber-toothed tigers, and also dogs, horses, monkeys, and apes. Some few of those apes descended from the trees and stood up for a better view. We humans have been seeking that clearer perspective ever since.

Life cascades—from the stardust and supernovae that are our heritage, whose elements compose our blood, bones, skin, and brains; whose electricity powers our nerves and consciousness. All of the cosmos is our mother/father; we are the descendants and the cousins of the galaxies. We are also the children and brothers and sisters and cousins of all living things, without exception. Everything everywhere is an expression of oneness. This is both scientific fact—inescapable and inspiring—and theological value—to be is to belong is to be community. Our oneness with all creation impels us to recognize community with all creation. God's oneness is expressed through creaturely solidarity and com/passion for all.

God and Creation: At Home in the World

Rather than looking for God in some supernatural realm removed from—or in opposition to—the oneness permeating the living cosmos, our explorations invite us back home, to recognize God as the super, natural one![3] God is found pervading nature's richness, disturbing the still predictability of entropy with eddies and whirls of increasing order, such as to bubble into rivulets of organization and life, which wash into a mindfulness that transcends species and erupts into awareness and self-awareness.

That fecund awareness is one of both boundary breaking *and* of uniqueness, simultaneously. Creation theology is iconoclastic—where some would establish distinctions, our embodied creatureliness also invites commonality across division. As the modern philosopher Hans Jonas tells us:

> The *continuity* of descent linking man with the animal world made it henceforth impossible to regard his mind, and mental phenomena in general, as the abrupt intrusion of an ontologically alien principle in the total stream of life. Man's isolation, the last citadel of dualism, disappeared, and he could once again use his knowledge of himself to interpret the totality of which he was a part.[4]

We are all stardust. Seeing all creation as phenomenologically diverse yet ontologically one invites a celebration of the relatedness of all natural events, including each of us and all of us, including the pervasive holiness that lures us to advance. This evolving emergence of growing complexity never violates the constraints of physics and its component parts. From its very inception, all life emerges from prior life, and life itself emerges from the organic and the nonbiological, so that all of creation is part of a single web, a single interconnected, related, growing process in which there seems to be a rise in complexity, experience, and ultimately perception and consciousness. As the mid-twentieth-century rabbi and thinker Milton Steinberg notes:

> The entire universe, as I see it, is the outward manifestation of Mind-energy, of Spirit, or to use the older and better word, of God. God is then the essential Being of all beings, though all beings in their totality do not exhaust Him. It is His reason which expressed itself in the rationality of nature, in the fact that all things behave in conformity with intelligible forms, in the fact, in brief, that the world is cosmos not chaos.[5]

When we connect with other living things, we tap into a relationship created by shared origins, common organization, overlapping responses to this wonderful planet. Anyone who has ever loved a pet, stood in awe at the shore of the sea as dolphins frolicked, marveled in wonder as salmon returned to their birthplaces in the latest cycle of death and life, stood in silence near a deer frozen in alert attentiveness, or even peered into a microscope at a simple bacterium and reflected on our common cellularity can attest to the profound inviting power of our commonality. Creation invites, "Halleluyah!"

Mind Your Matter: Consciousness All the Way Down

A creation theology takes seriously that emergent evolution simultaneously highlights continuity and discontinuity. Rare are those aspects of nature that do not have some earlier, simpler expression at a more fundamental level. As Jonas describes it, "We can see everything surpassing animality as a new stage of mediate relationship to the world that is already beginning to take form in animals and, in turn, is already based upon the mediate nature of all organic existence as such."[6] Even as a phenomenon can reach toward novelty, it does so on the shoulder of its emergent context. So it is with inwardness, subjectivity, mindfulness, and consciousness, which some take to be the defining traits of humanity, our unique and exclusive prerogative. One need not embrace a full-blown panpsychism (that everything has some degree of awareness and self-determination) to recognize the roots of mindfulness far down to the simplest levels of creation, and scientific evidence is extending mindfulness to the very earliest levels of the biosphere, perhaps even beyond. In the words of Milton Steinberg:

> His power moves in the dynamisms of physical reality. His will is the impulse behind the upsurge of life on this planet. Individualized, He is the soul of man whose thought processes are infinitesimal sparks of His infinite fire, whose moral aspirations are fragments of His vast purpose, whose yearning to create is but an echo of His cosmic creativity. And He is an ethical being, not so much in the sense that He enters into relations with His own expressions, as in the

deeper sense that He is the fountainhead, source, and sanction of man's moral life. The human quest after freedom,
truth, goodness, and beauty is but the splintered spearhead
of the divine drive. So to me, the whole panorama of earth
and sky, the tempestuous progress of living things, and the
tortuous career of humanity, are the external shell of a process wherein God realizes His character.[7]

A few examples will suffice to suggest a more pervasive and richer
sense of mindfulness for the entire cosmos and its creatures. (Note
that in each case, I am citing cases that went against what experts
"knew" of the life-form's capability and that I am "descending" the
ladder of evolution with each example.)

- Reports of a chimp that prove that nonhuman primates plan for
  the future, in this case by stockpiling rocks during the night to
  fling at unwelcome human visitors at the Furuvik Zoo in Sweden.[8]

- The parrot Alex, who broke through a series of presumed limits
  on what birds allegedly could learn: "Birds cannot learn to label
  objects, they said. Alex did. OK, birds cannot learn to generalize. Alex did. All right, but they cannot learn concepts. Alex did.
  Well, they certainly cannot understand 'same' versus 'different.'
  Alex did."[9]

- Rooks, Eurasian members of the crow family, were able to spontaneously learn to cooperate to move a platform, with each bird
  tugging on an end of a rope simultaneously to make it possible
  to get the food on the platform.[10]

- Two neuroethologists, from the University of Toulouse and
  Australian National University in Canberra, taught free-flying
  bees to track a trail of colored marks, which they were then able
  to do in a completely unfamiliar maze. They learned to demonstrate delayed matching-to-sample (DMTS) and were able to
  generalize to situations never previously encountered, learning
  an abstract relation.[11]

- A team of Japanese researchers from Hokkaido University demonstrated that *Physarum* slime-mold amoebas demonstrate the ability to memorize and anticipate repeated events. The study showed

"a primitive version of brain function" in an organism that has no brain! Biophysicist Toshiyuki Nakagaki noted that this finding "might be a chance to reconsider what intelligence is."[12]

For Hans Jonas, "Whether we give this inwardness the name of feeling, receptiveness, response to stimuli, volition, or something else—it harbors, in some degree of 'awareness,' the absolute interest of the organism in its own being, agency, and continuation."[13] Human consciousness may feel particularly precious, and rightly so. But it is also part of a broader phenomenon that extends across living things, beginning with responses to stimuli that move toward self-preservation and pleasure and away from death and pain. Mindfulness appears to pervade creation, fashioned of the same stuff as humans are. It may differ in kind, but it shares a resistance to obliteration and sameness that is found in matter as well as throughout the biosphere. Matter, it seems, is neither inert nor brute. It upwells in a rich range of characteristics, responses, reactions, and finally in living things, to intentions and self-awareness.

Free to Be You and Me

We are a part of nature. Yet we are also distinctive, aware of our own awareness, living with an intensity and complexity of feeling and reflection that we do not find in the same degree elsewhere in our natural family. Same yet different, related yet distinct, as we ponder our cousins in creation our awareness of marvel is simultaneously an awareness of our distinctiveness. Only a distinctive creature could summon feelings of marvel, relationship, and connection. And only a particularly mindful creature could think about the wonder of such thoughts and choose to act on them. In true dipolar fashion, a creation theology bids us to acknowledge both our embedded commonality and our distinctive uniqueness. Creation asks of us to say, "Amen!" and to choose. An embodied theology of creation invites its children to partake of freedom, to actualize real agency.

Freedom and Agency—Creatures' and Creator's

Everything Participates in Choosing the Future

> Going free is comparable to a renewal of the world.
> —Rabbi Abraham ibn Ezra to Exodus 21:6

At the core of the human experience of life is freedom and free will, the ability to have real choices and a capacity to distinguish among options to select a preferred action without coercion. This includes the coercion that the next step constitutes the necessary response to the previous cause. We act as though we are free—selecting what to wear, how to work, with whom to live, how to recreate, what to eat and when. Even those philosophers, theologians, and scientists whose intellectual apparatus denies freedom as illusory or merely as apparent conduct themselves as though they are free. They even hold others accountable for the actions they do not condone, despite their theoretical denial of self-determination in freedom. In many ways free will is also a necessary component—to a greater or lesser degree of self-awareness—for living things, and even for nonliving natural events, to respond in ways that preserve their distinct characteristics or properties. Agency seems fundamental to self-identity; and agency, by definition, is free.

That same freedom and free will anchors systems of law, morality and ethics, reward and punishment. Without the capacity to make free choices, without the ability to choose how to act (or not) and to know what the consequences may be, it would be unjustifiable to make moral demands or to punish improper behavior. Only the capacity to choose the good justifies holding the perpetrator accountable. That same cornerstone of freedom supports the entire scaffold of education and commandment, each of which presumes freedom and the need to learn and practice goodness as rehearsal for life itself. There is much to say about the centrality of free will and agency again under the rubric of revelation, but at present our concern is what freedom means in the context of creation.

Are We Free, or Are We Deluded?

Dominant theologies straddle a delicate—some might say untenable—line on this issue. In the words of Rabbi Akiva, "All is foreseen, yet freedom of choice is given" (*Mishnah Avot* 3:15). While insisting that God is all-knowing and all-powerful, hence absolutely aware and in control of all that ever was and all that will ever be, many authorities of Western traditions also insist on limited room for human free will if only to justify reward and punishment, commandedness or salvation. As Maimonides explains:

> Were a person compelled to act according to the dictates of predestination, then the commands and prohibitions of the Law would become null and void and the Law would be completely false, since a person would have no freedom of choice in action. Moreover, it would be useless, in fact absolutely in vain, for a person to study, to instruct, or attempt to learn an art, as it would be entirely impossible, on account of the external force compelling action, according to the opinion of those who hold this view, to keep from doing a certain act, from gaining certain knowledge, or from acquiring a certain characteristic. Reward and punishment, too, would be pure injustice.[1]

Maimonides, reflecting many other theologians, appears to justify the conflict between absolute divine foreknowledge and human freedom to choose by distinguishing God's knowing as radically different from human knowing, and affirming God's foreknowledge and control of natural events in contradistinction to human choice.[2] Because God is the knower, the process of knowing, and the thing known simultaneously, somehow God's absolute "knowing" is mysteriously compatible with human freedom.[3] Most theologians leave it at that—what contemporary philosopher and theologian Philip Clayton chillingly labels "a rationality-stultifying appeal to mystery."[4]

Many physicists avoid this unstable dichotomy by espousing a determinism inspired by their scientistic metaphysics: that free will is illusory, that all matter is explicable ultimately by its component parts that operate according to fixed laws, so that each new action is simply the consequence of the sum total of previous actions leading to that moment in an unbroken chain. We may still lack the ability for perfect predictability, but this is not held to be a flaw in determinism, but rather a reflection of insufficient information or of excessive complexity. Some biologists advocate determinism in the biological realm as well, either because of a reductionist acceptance that biological behavior is rooted in—and determined by—its physical components or because of a belief that genetic endowments dictate particular results.

Yet, We Do Choose!

Of course, not all scientists espouse determinism.[5] As we now are capable of recognizing the "laws" of the cosmos themselves as emergent generalizations of the behavior and patterns of natural events, specific details of how evolution unfolds need not be preordained, no mere filling in a predesigned tapestry.[6] Instead, the ways the patterns express as shorthand a dynamic and shifting cosmos, life, and consciousness are very much selected with feedback from the characteristics and responses of the elements themselves, by the coalescing into stars and galaxies with particular dimensions, composition, and velocities, by particular life-forms deciding to live, eat, and copulate in specific places with particular individuals in particular ways. The actions of the creatures shape the specific contours of evolving reality no less than the emergent patterns constrain their outcome and interaction. There is actual selecting in natural selection.

Honoring the agency of natural entities blurs the lines between evolution and creation and between primary evolutionary "goals" and spandrels. Evolution is clearly not a planned process, in which from the very first moment, every single goal was intended, specified, mapped, and slowly attained, as some religious devotees may have mistakenly presumed. But neither is it simply the mechanistic, directionless unfolding of happenstance, as some scientistic materialists would insist. Rather, evolution and life become, with increasing effectiveness, partners in the ongoing, open-ended process of creation.[7] One can speak of creation itself as being a co-creative process and that divinity, in some aspects, is the creative impulse to be found in, with, and through the natural process—unbalancing equilibrium, stimulating creativity, producing novelty, encouraging relationship. Biological entities are choosing, willing, designing entities. With their own emerging complexity, their intentionality and freedom increase as well.

None of this precludes an overarching teleology, a Final Cause, to borrow a fecund Aristotelian category, not as guaranteed outcome, but as aspiration and object of yearning—by the cosmos, by its creatures, by the Creator. In other words, the details might be ad hoc responses every step of the way, but it sure looks like the universe arcs toward consciousness, relationship, complexity. Stephen Jay Gould, a paleontologist at Harvard, and Richard Lewontin, a population geneticist, may well be right in their description of the proximate cause of the so-called spandrel's (the unintended space above the lintel and under the arch in a church) beginnings, but science as method properly ignores final causes, teleology, purpose, because such purposiveness is not measurable, not subject to test, not empirical. That system-driven ignoring of ultimate purpose doesn't prove that there are no ultimate causes, no final goal. It just means that for science to work, we can't talk or think about that possibility. In a similar way, if we are analyzing the chemistry of Van Gogh's blue paint, we can't have a discussion about his brushstrokes or even what the painting portrays. Those are simply different levels of conversation, and blurring them together would make any real analysis impossible. To exclude in principle what a method disregards methodologically is to confuse an extremely useful procedure for a metaphysical assertion, impossible to verify or refute.

Transcending dichotomies of "either/or" (coincidence /significant), we can—in good dipolar fashion—affirm "both/and." As proximate cause, a particular development may well have originated as a spandrel—the secondary by-product of a beneficial selection. (It is now held, for example, that the complex parts of a sperm's tail evolved initially for other multiple and unrelated purposes. At some stage, these separate developments were brought together and drafted for the attainment of better mobility by sperm that gained significant evolutionary advantage.) But what began as a spandrel may acquire—precisely because of its availability—significance and utility after the fact: initially, spandrel; eventually, survival enhancing and life affirming (those sperm tails now propel the eager sperm toward a happy union!). Science is methodologically mute as to the question of any general intentionality (final cause) lurking under the surface of natural events (proximate and material causes). But that doesn't mean the cosmos isn't purposive.

Creation in the Mode of Freedom

This affirmation of the possibility of purpose brings us to the theological question of divine action, free will, and purpose. Having rejected a materialist reductionism, we are not constrained to contain our explanation exclusively into the Procrustean bed of physical cause and effect, although we remain committed to providing a broader context consistent with scientific knowledge and explanation. Having demonstrated the shortcomings of dominant theologies as factually literal descriptions, with their assertions of a supernatural deity outside of time and space, omniscient and omnipotent, exercising coercive force on passive substances and capable of suspending the "laws" of nature, we are now free to explore the ways that divinity actually might work with, through, and in nature on behalf of enhanced life, novelty, relationship, justice, and joy. Creation beckons, both as event and as process. As part of that ongoing process, as heir to every prior attainment of creation, we can look in and out to articulate what freedom and agency might mean in a world of wondrous complexity, novelty, and relationship.

Creation, in all of the diverse ways that it has been understood, has consistently nested in freedom. Twentieth-century theologian Abraham Joshua Heschel points out, "The essential meaning of creation is, as Maimonides explained, the idea that the universe did not come about by necessity but as a result of freedom."[8] Whether we speak of the event of creation—big bang or the emergence of bubbles of order in an infinite sea of quantum uncertainty—or the ongoing process of continual creation (co-creation, really), the cornerstone for integrating our sense of ourselves as products and participants in the unfolding of creation is freedom. We find ourselves capable of making choices, of those choices bearing consequences for which we are responsible and which form the ground and constraint (and sometimes, goad) for subsequent choices. Human consciousness is self-evidently an act of freedom—the decision to pursue a particular activity, to invest in a specific relationship, to cultivate a distinct virtue, or to indulge a special vice. At each moment, as we continue becoming a singular instantiation of our self, we choose from the potential possibilities available at that moment, and it is *our* decision that elevates one possibility among several into an objective reality, an event. As Heschel notes, "The grand premise of religion is that man is able to surpass himself. Such ability is the essence of freedom."[9]

Taking seriously our own embodied reality as a manifestation of nature's potential, recognizing our own vitality, dynamism, and consciousness as emergent expressions of the cosmos itself, we recognize that any description of reality that excludes consciousness, choice, freedom is a gerrymandered explanation—partial at best, deceptive at worst. The fullest possible description of the world is one that integrates all natural entities, including our dynamic and persistent expression of free will and choice. If that choice is fundamental to a full description of nature, it is also reasonable to recognize that same freedom in the divinity that permeates, grounds, and manifests as the continuing work of creation. Like God's creation, God is dynamic and free.

God's Freedom, the Universe's, and Ours

It is for this reason that Jewish traditions of creation, for all their diversity, recognize and insist that God as Creator was and is free, that God's creating is an expression of the same freedom that we, made in God's image, bring to our task of becoming, of co-creating a universe of justice, love, and peace. To recognize that God's creation is free is to recognize that God creates truly—existence and becoming are not illusory, nor are they a reflection of a distorted perspective. Creation is real. God does not *have* to create a cosmos; existent reality does not emerge inevitably.

Creation reflects divine choice, commitment, and gift. Creation is choice because there is nothing necessary or inevitable about this world, this physics, or this consciousness. It did not have to develop this particular way, and slight shifts in fundamental forces, happenstance, natural or voluntary selection at any stage in the process would have invited irretrievably different outcomes. Creation is a commitment, setting a process in motion that brooks no interference and tolerates no gaps. The decision to create creatures is a decision for there to be consequences for the nature out of which they grow and which they impact in turn. Those creatures now share in the power of making choices, of having impact, of determining outcomes. God gives us a gift by making the commitment to be Creator.

Creation is a gift, made evident by the way that we and all living things cling to life as the most precious of gifts, and we seek to share it with our offspring and enhance it with communities of our own species as well as with other living creatures.

A choice, a commitment, and a gift, the processes of creation are real; they have abiding, ongoing significance and exercise real agency. For God to choose to create means necessarily for God to share power, irrevocably and without retraction. To create means neither more nor less than to establish the parameters in which a new, significant entity can emerge. Recall that we have conceived ontological realism as the capacity to cause effects, to have an impact. By that definition, the emergence of space-time, of cosmological entities that in turn created possibilities of stars, solar systems, planets, and on (at least) one planet, life itself are processes that are established and abiding. To claim that God is really the Creator, yet to hold that creation is illusory or lacks real agency is a self-contradiction—to create means to create real independence.

Having chosen to create means that God is no longer the sole existent or the totality of power. The reality of creation is an eruption of partnership—of multiple centers of agency in addition to the Divine, of other centers of will in addition to God's. Creation means that there are other agendas besides the divine agenda. The triumph of God's will is no longer assured, because the only way to guarantee that end would be to have never created other loci of will in the first place. Entering into the welter of time and relationship creates both a dynamism and a vulnerability that does not exist in eternity. Dominant theology shows its internal contradiction by simultaneously seeking to hold God as Creator while in significant measure denying the reality of the very act of creation. Becoming Creator means renouncing the monopoly of power as creatures now exercise power on their own.

Recognizing that the components and participants in creation also manifest agency means that God now works with, in, and through the agencies that God has created, is creating, and will create. It is not that everything is divine, which would be equivalent to saying that nothing is divine, or that whatever happens reflects God's will. Creation is the sharing of agency: "I have put before you life and death, blessing and curse. Choose life" (Deuteronomy 30:19). God has organized the process of creation so that created entities themselves have a say in the continuing process of creation: "Why was this world created through the letter *hei*/ה? Because the world is like an exedra [which, like the letter *hei*, is closed on three sides, open on one]. You may go out [astray] if you wish" (Talmud, *Menachot* 29b). God has taken a great risk—the vulnerability that other agencies may overwhelm divine agency, that God's creatures and creation may not turn toward the divine lure, may not attune themselves to God's invitation and call. It may well be that we, creaturely entities, may not rise to the divine optimum. We may give in to our exhaustion, pettiness, insecurity, greed, drives, or ambitions and not make the effort to rise to inclusion, justice, and love. We may sink into the somnambulance of self-satisfaction rather than reach for the rigors of relatedness. In the words of the Midrash, "God does not predetermine whether a person shall be righteous or wicked. That God leaves to the person to decide."[10] As risky as such an outcome may be, a cosmos created is one that chooses its own way. God's will be done is a worthy aspiration and an abiding possibility. Whether or not it is achieved, however, is our decision as free creatures, to be made along with the rest of creation.

What Is God's Role in Creation?

What is God doing with God's freedom and ours? In good bipolar fashion, there are two broad answers to this question—from the perspective of eternity, and from within the dynamism of space-time. The perspective of eternity is one of logical necessity and possibility. Beyond the realm of relationship, eternity establishes the parameters of what may become but is itself beyond becoming. Like the Kabbalah's transcendent *Ein Sof* (without end), God eternally and objectively remains the repository of every event that has ever happened, of every creature who has ever existed. What is once real is eternally, objectively real in God's mind. Also in the eternal realm,

God is the source of all potentiality and every possibility wafting from the future toward the coming-into-being of the dynamic present. As logical necessity and infinite potential, God is beyond space-time, beyond relationship, beyond knowledge. This is the aspect of God as potent silence, as all-embracing No/thing, as the sea of infinite, eternal quantum fluctuation. Of this aspect of God, little can be said or known literally; this is the realm of the five M's: math, metaphor, meditation, myth, and music. Of God's eternity, we can only anticipate and intuit.

But there is another aspect to the Divine, that aspect that enters into relationship, into vulnerability, into time and space. That aspect of God is dynamic and open to change, as is the creation that is generated by this new dynamism. This second mode is made possible in kabbalistic terms through *tzimtzum* (withdrawal, contraction, constriction). In the mythic language of Kabbalah, God as infinite/eternal contracts to a single point that explodes into creation—all space-time and all becoming—or, alternatively, *tzimtzum* creates a sphere of emptiness into which divine light then erupts into space-time and becoming. This process of becoming is embodied, temporal, and dynamic. In such a mode, all is related to all, and lower orders emerge from higher orders. This process of emergence is portrayed either as a sphere with spheres inside it or as a Tree of Life, in which the manifestations of divine relating are depicted as hierarchical and as spilling out one from the other, top to bottom. It is this dynamic, relating aspect of God that enters into relationship with, in, and through creation, intuited, known, and covenanted. This becoming is God as active process, as ground of novelty and creating, as impulse to relate, care, rectify, and nurture. This is God as known in the dynamism of our space-time bubble. Of this relational aspect of God, we well up in song and prayer, in learning and in *mitzvot*, in love and deeds of *chesed*, lovingkindness: "The world is built on love" (Psalm 89:3). We can think, and speak, and do.

Meeting God, and Ourselves, in Creation

At every moment, at every level, God meets us where we are, as we are, and offers us the best possible choice to be made at that moment. Recognizing the constraints of the past leading up to this moment, the record of our previous choices and character, the ways that others have impinged on our possibilities—and opened up doors, too—we see divinity as holding the potentialities that are available at that juncture, of urging, inviting, and beckoning us to make the best possible choice—the choice that enhances our ability to relate, love, include, and grow. God is offering that call at every moment, but also at every level—to subatomic particles, to stars and galaxies, to all created entities, all living things: cells, systems, creatures, communities, planet. As the Midrash notes, "There is no blade of grass that grows without having a *mazal* [guiding star]... telling it to grow" (*Genesis Rabbah* 10:6). At every moment, as the continuous work of creation advances, God invites all as co-creators to extend our efforts toward advancement of greater justice, greater connection, greater interaction, greater experience, greater love. The lure toward innovation, toward creativity and risk, toward caring and belonging is the call that we recognize as God's agency.[11] And we meet that call with our own decision to integrate that invitation into the objective reality of our becoming at that moment, or not.

In the same way that God is meeting us at every moment and every level with the invitation toward the best possible choice, we in turn meet all of creation and every moment leading up to this moment, integrating all past choices into our own becoming in the present, and intuitively expressing the totality of creation welling up in each moment of our choosing to become. This consciousness of interrelated belonging is a powerful resource for deepening inner life and activism in the world, as expressed by Rabbi Nachman of Breslov:

> Majesty of Space-time! Grant me the ability to be alone. May it be my custom to go outdoors each day among the trees and

the grass—among all growing entities—and there may I be
alone, and enter into prayer, to talk with the One to whom I
belong. There may I express everything in my heart, and may
all the foliage of the field—all grasses, trees, and plants—
awaken at my arrival, to send the powers of their life into the
words of my prayer so that my prayer and speech are made
whole through the life and spirit of all growing things, which
are made as one by their transcendent Source.[12]

We are, at this moment, the integration of all of evolutionary history—
cosmic and biological—to this very time. And we integrate that totality
of belonging—the entire past and all else that exists contemporaneously
with us—into the becoming that selects and embodies one possibility
of our potential. This act of selecting and enacting is both a limitation
(some of what was once possible is no longer) and a culmination (what
was once merely potential is now actual and objectively real forever).
As modern philosopher Hans Jonas has reminded us, biological organisms represent a great leap in the capacity of nature to organize, transmit, and select information. That emergent capability comes together
as novel modes of being—freedom of movement, perception, and feeling.[13] With each new emergent capacity, a new ability to engage the
rest of the world and a deepening interiority also enter into becoming.
Animal life awakens into sentience, into perception, appetite, drive, and
fear. This greater engagement, paradoxically, expresses a sense of growing differentiation. The more complex the animal, the more acutely it
perceives itself in distinction to its surroundings, its fellow creatures, its
bliss. To bridge this chasm requires decision, risk, and action. Animal
life is, as Jonas reminds, passionate life.

This Risk (and Glory) of Freedom

The freedom that erupts in living things is no Pollyannaish utopia.
Freedom entails the challenge of maintaining identity, of survival.
Living entities maintain their identities by competing for scarce
resources, by ingesting other living entities, by displacing others.
The emergence of living entities introduced the distinction between

life and death, a form of nonbeing that could only exist with the introduction of living. Metabolism, then, created the dichotomy of being and nonbeing, and the relentless struggle against nonbeing, a struggle that had not existed until the emergence of life.[14] Metabolizing creatures have influence and capacities, but they also have needs and necessities. In poetic language, Jonas offers that the "nature of lifeless matter would be interpreted as sleeping, not yet awakened freedom."[15] As matter awakened into emergent freedom, it simultaneously awakened to the task and opportunity of self-integrating and self-sustaining. Terror and elation, joy and struggle are made possible and necessary by the ongoing becoming that is life. To be free is to live with great risk. As Process philosopher Alfred North Whitehead observes, "At the heart of the nature of things, there are always the dream of youth and the harvest of tragedy. The Adventure of the Universe starts with a dream and reaps tragic beauty."[16]

With each increase in complexity, life expands both its capacity to risk and to achieve, to experience joy, gratification, achievement, and also pain, terror, and suffering. These different experiences are inextricably linked to levels of consciousness and awareness and are impossible except as a total package. One cannot be free without risking pain and loss. One cannot acquire the consciousness that savors a grandchild without also knowing the pain of a loved one's suffering or demise. One cannot respond with awe to the starry heavens without having the capacity to respond with terror to the possibilities of social injustice or planetary extinction. Heightened consciousness entails greater sensitivity, both pleasant and terrible; the capacity to suffer and to exult expands with the capacity to comprehend and self-reflect. As the One who holds all suffering and rejoicing objectively and eternally, God is the most moved mover; in Alfred North Whitehead's words, "God is the great companion—the fellow sufferer who understands."[17] The Rabbis, similarly, prehend, "*Aluf* [companion] refers to the Holy Blessing One, as it says, 'You are the companion of my youth' (Jeremiah 3:4)" (Talmud, *Chagigah* 17b).

Creation, then, is both event and process. As event, we recall the beginning of beginnings coyly peaking from behind the veil of knowledge, forever teasing us with its unreachable allure. Prior to Planck time, that brief interval right after the big bang when the infant cosmos was so dense and hot that the regularities of physics had not yet kicked in, before knowing was possible, before time was time, in a place where place was not yet, *Bereishit*, the beginning, marks an axiomatic eruption—axiomatic in that itself it remains inexplicable. (Many untestable theories abound in the discourse of scientists, straining to extend the scientific worldview beyond the limits of its own method, and in the dream talk of mystics, yearning to engage the ineffable in the symbol dance of their song.) In this age of bleak dichotomies, we are told to choose between two incompatible tellings: the spontaneous creation out of nothing of all space, time, and matter either in an instantaneous creation of all that currently exists or in an infinite quantum sea of uncertainty that produces rare bubbles of relatively stable space-time in which universes can develop spontaneously. Neither telling can prove its own veracity empirically. There are no experiments in which we can run bubbling universes out of quantum eternity or goad an omnipotent creator into fashioning a solitary cosmos like this one.

But we are not reduced to selecting which fundamentalism will possess us. There is a third way—a way of integration, imagination, and pluralism. Just as different modes of knowing pertain at different levels of emergence, so different ways of telling can communicate aspects of creation and its abiding value for our own living and becoming. The process of creation moves us, in us, and through us. And we, throughout our short becomings, move creation a bit. Embracing all, we make ourselves co-creators with God and cosmos in a universe in process. As creation's self-reflective expression, our truest turn, and greatest challenge, is to cultivate the virtue of gratitude.

To Life!

A Cosmic *Dayenu*

For how many good deeds are we obligated to God!...
Had God split the sea for us, but not
brought us to dry land ...
Had God provided for our needs ...
but not provided manna,
Dayenu—It would have been sufficient!
—The Passover Haggadah

Both an emotion and a goad to behavior, gratitude holds our attention in awe and thanks at the startling chain of blessings and fortuities that allowed us to reach this day and, in good dipolar fashion, propels us forward with an agenda of hope and love. We are aware of our embodied belonging, of being an extension of an evolutionary process stretching back to the very beginnings of time. Heirs to billions of years of fortuity, choice, complexification, and emergence, we focus our consciousness on ourselves and then on the cosmos of which we are a part. How could we respond other than with delight, dismay, resolve, and ultimately gratitude, a sense of having been gifted something extravagant, unlikely, and privileged?[1]

In Jewish liturgy, one of the most popular songs, *"Dayenu,"* sung at the Passover seder, celebrates a series of miracles, any of which would have been more than sufficient.[2] The song opens with a Hebrew line that exults: "For how many good deeds are we obligated to God!" The miracles start with a cluster of five acts taking us out of slavery, then a second cluster of five miracles, and finally a cluster of five events transforming the Jews into a covenant people. At the mention of each miracle, the assembled guests sing, "*Dayenu*—it would have been sufficient!" The Hebrew of the opening line offers us an enticing invitation to play on a cosmic level: *Kamah ma'alot tovot La-Makom aleinu!* The Hebrew word used for God is *Ha-Makom* (the Place), and the term for good deeds is *ma'alot tovot; ma'aleh* is an ascension, a stair, an increase, a revelation. *Aleinu* can mean "we are obligated" or "upon us." "With how many beneficent emergences has the Place—our cosmos—obligated us!"

Appropriately, the traditional "*Dayenu*" ends with an evocative call to gratitude: *Al achat kamah ve-khamah tovah khefulah u-mekhufelet la-Makom aleinu.* Conventionally translated "How much more so are we obligated to God!" this strange terminology lures us toward a playful cosmic expression. *Achat* is "one," and *al achat kamah ve-khamah* is "what a statistical fluke and long shot"; *khefulah* is "doubled," and *mekhufelet* is "redoubled." So we wind up with an exclamation of wonder and thanks: "With what extraordinarily unlikely good has the Place obligated us!"

The list that follows invokes a cosmic/biological *dayenu*. Had any one of these wonders occurred alone, it would have been extraordinary (although unnoted, since conscious life required every step *in toto*). Yet each one did occur, and lined up in such a way that continuous evolution became possible. Out of this shaky ladder of unlikely events, there emerged sufficient stability, creativity, and fine-tuning for life to emerge, and out of life, consciousness. To express consciousness, so rare among all matter, would be gift enough. To possess the requisite tools—intellectual, technological—to know something about the world and the cosmos, to live in that fleeting time in which we are sufficiently complex, the cosmos is sufficiently compact, and our knowledge sufficiently advanced is astounding, miraculous. *Dayenu!* This trifecta will not come again because:

- We live in that most rare of all possibilities—a long-lived universe. Some physicists work backward from the present to the big bang and theorize that cosmic inflation is the eternal state of existence.[3] The world of eternal inflation is a quantum realm, as nothing can get any bigger because it is always inflating away from all other events too quickly to even approach atomic size. This realm is constantly creative, and the notions of time and space have no meaning, as there is no direction or change over time and there are no variations or entities to create space. This realm is infinite potential—nothing persists, nothing is realized. But out of this eternally writhing creative potential there are rare emergences of bubbles in which inflation stops. We live in such a miraculous anomaly—time has direction, space has distinction, galaxies emerge, and life evolves. *Dayenu!*

- We live in a remarkably fine-turned space-time bubble, perfect for the emergence of conscious life. Whether one chooses to admit the possibility of an eternal quantum fluctuation or restricts one's gaze to the empirically testable space-time bubble in which we live, the fact remains that the cosmos is extraordinarily precise in the adjustment of its major forces and their interactions such that emergent life and consciousness are possible, despite being such a statistical long shot. *Dayenu!*

- We living things are stardust (and hydrogen), matter so rare— dark energy constitutes about 70 percent of the matter in the universe, cold dark matter another 25 percent, invisible atoms 4 percent, hydrogen and helium another 0.5 percent. The stardust of which we are made constitutes a mere 0.01 percent of all matter, but it takes this entire pyramid of matter to produce the startling complexity that is life and consciousness. As astronomer Alan Dressler exults, "If we could but learn to look at the universe with eyes that are blind to power and size, but keen for subtlety and complexity, then our world would outshine a galaxy of stars."[4] Surely that constitutes grounds for gratitude. *Dayenu!*

- We are living in the center of time—neither too early nor too late, it is just right. At an age of approximately fourteen billion years, the cosmos is old enough to have emerged into consciousness, yet young enough that the dark matter has not overwhelmed visible matter or spread matter so far apart that no light/radiation can beam information to the earth. We have been around long enough to develop the capacity to read the information coming to us—the first generation to have empirical knowledge about the earliest moments of our cosmos. Earlier in time, this information would have remained in code, unreadable. In the future, because of the dominance of dark energy and matter and the continuing expansion of space, it will be too scattered to retrieve. We live in the center of time, just right to know our home and to celebrate it. *Dayenu*!

- Our size is the central size possible—neither too big, nor too small, we are just right. As we explored above, living things are the central size, midway between the very largest (the cosmic horizon itself) and the very smallest (Planck length). Humans are at the center of this size distribution—about the size necessary for the complexity of consciousness to emerge, yet small enough for electricity to deliver information in a sufficiently timely fashion. *Dayenu*!

- Of all the places in the vast space-time bubble, earth is unusually— perhaps uniquely—suitable for the emergence of life. Our solar system's circular orbits, quite rare among galaxies, are necessary to provide the stability that complex life requires. The larger planets have shielded the earth from comets and stabilized our orbit. The earth finds itself in the small habitable zone— far enough for water to remain liquid without evaporating or freezing—and has been so for most of its history, giving life sufficient time to evolve. A thin planetary crust and active tectonics have kept carbon and other essential elements in circulation, and the fortuitous/cataclysmic crash of a proto-planet that created our oversized moon has kept the tilt of the earth's rotation axis constant, providing stable seasons and tides that have slowed the earth's rotation. Finally, our solar system lies in the narrow range of a galactic habitable zone. This concatenation of unlikely events made it possible for the emergence of conscious life on earth. *Dayenu*!

- The emergence of intelligent life from prokaryotes took 999/1,000 of the earth's age. A series of breaks—lucky for us, unfortunate for others—continued to contribute to the development of complex life. On earth, we are unaware of any other, separate launching of life; it appears that life started once and that all life is related to all previous life, continuously. That makes the adventure of emergent complexity in living things fragile, unlikely, and extraordinary. *Dayenu!*

- The human brain is the universe's most complex and wondrous entity. With over thirty billion nerve cells and one million billion connections, the number of possible pathways far exceeds the number of elementary particles in the known universe.[5] Each cubic millimeter of cerebral cortex contains roughly one billion synapses. Its complexity is so vast that it operates uniquely to be conscious, self-conscious, and able to regulate conscious and unconscious operations at the same time. Our identities, memories, and awareness all emerge as brain-based functioning, and there is no comparable complexity we know of. No two brains are alike, and each evolves beyond its genetic inheritance by a feedback loop responding to the unique experiences and thoughts of the particular individual. The workings of the human brain, the process that is each mind, is unique, private, world-changing, world-creating, self-creating, and world-enhancing. *Dayenu!*

With what extraordinarily improbable successions of events have we emerged! How wondrous the evolution of self-organizing matter into life and consciousness! How vast our gratitude at this improbable and wondrous turn of events! How much is gratitude incumbent upon us as an expression of our marvel and our thanks!

Part III

CREATION IN SPACE AND TIME

God's festivals require the sanctification of the
Court, but the Shabbat, which honors creation, does
not require sanctification by the Court.
—Babylonian Talmud, *Nedarim* 78b

Enlightened by a renewed integration of science and spirit, we enter into a cosmos that is dynamic, relational, and open. We have an active role in making real a particular possibility of the future, as does every other event in creation, and we know that our becoming is an ongoing process that responds and helps contribute to the becoming of every other creature and all creation.

In this section we mobilize that enriched view of nature to explore what that means for our sense of time and space, focusing specifically on a Jewish and biblical understanding of creation as the ongoing invitation of chaos to become cosmos. That continuous lure of the *tohu va-vohu* (chaos) and the *tehom* (deep) into *olam* (cosmos) is the steady work of the Divine, a work to which we are invited as participants no less than as recipients.

Judaism's central encounter with the rhythms of time is through the calendar, marking the seasons and the cycle of holy days and festivals that renew our experience of miraculous moments and pivotal events. Rather than being a hodgepodge of random memories, the year is structured to flow with deliberation between the pillar of historical memories of salvation and revelation and the pillar of cosmic and individual occasions for creation, re-creation, and renewal. With this section, we will do the work of integrating our enriched scientific sense of nature's marvels, a Judaism founded on freedom and relationship, with a way of living that dynamic openness through the primary story of how things began and the ongoing journey through the year's pivotal observances and celebrations.

Vibrating over the Face of the Deep

Continuous Creation and Jewish Faithfulness

> When God began creating the heavens and the earth,
> —the earth was chaos, and dark was on
> the face of the deep,
> and the wind of God vibrated on
> the face of the waters—
> God said, "Let there be light!"
> —Genesis 1:1–3

At this point, our consideration of a creation theology must dip back for the most recent emergent reality: the cultural and religious heritage and ongoing creativity of human expression. In a dynamic, interactive loop, culture and spirit create the mental categories and cultural presuppositions that shape our scientific agenda, the questions we bring to research and the range of meanings we use to organize the data we discover. That scientific data, in turn, feeds back into our culture and our spirituality, modifying our view of ourselves and our cosmos, creating new metaphors and understandings of what it means to be, to live, to be human. This swirling interaction is mutually fructifying and challenging, and in the actual living, the two phases are inseparable. Culture frames the science that frames the culture that frames the science.

Recovering Creation

One cannot begin, then, at *the* beginning; one can only leap in where we find ourselves at present.[1] Our consideration of creation began by reviewing the rich harvest that scientific evidence has offered, as mediated through the cultural and religious openings of this age. Ours is a time in which dynamism, interrelatedness, and innovation entice the imagination, and our scientific understandings have benefited from these ways of speaking, organizing, and advancing what we know. Keeping our scientific harvest in hand, it is time to turn to the other source of creation material: the wealth of stories, poetry, and wisdom expressed in biblical and rabbinic scripture. One can subsume revelation as a subset of creation; after all, our stories and memories are part of the natural expression of human animals. One can equally view creation as under the rubric of revelation, known through our literature, mediated through our culture—"the Torah is only given in human language."[2] For this consideration, we seek to grasp the two poles of human becoming—creation as revelation *and* revelation as creation—without prioritizing or absolutizing either one. In the same way that both science and the humanities can benefit from a view of mutually influencing interaction, so too can creation and revelation. What we have explored in science—and philosophy—makes possible a renewed and liberating understanding of the biblical and rabbinic tellings. Our renewed philosophical, theological, and literary takes on the Jewish canons of creation can stimulate new possibilities in our integration of scientific understanding and its significance.

Back to a Beginning

Let us caress the Torah's emergent, embodied creation, one word at a time. While there are echoes of several mythic—and violent—creation tales scattered throughout the *Tanakh*, pride of place has been accorded to the opening chapters of the book of Genesis, and it is on that telling that we will focus. As Rashi so fetchingly observes of the Hebrew Bible's opening line, "This verse says nothing but, 'Expound me!'" Rich in layers of meanings, the resonant and spare theopoetics of Genesis invites us to swim in its swirling waters and exult in its emerging complexity and creativity.

We begin by noting that the very first word, *Bereishit*, invites engagement. Most English translations incorrectly (based on the King James translation) render the word as if it were an absolute, "In the beginning," implying that a Supernatural Being, God, created space, time, and all things *ex nihilo*, out of nothing.

At no point in the Hebrew Bible itself is a creation out of nothing explicitly affirmed, much less made a point of dogma. The first such clear reference is in apocryphal literature (2 Maccabees 7:28), although there are some passages in the Midrash that do seem to support *creatio ex nihilo* (*Genesis Rabbah* 1:9), and during the medieval and early modern periods, it was the dominant view for Jews as it was for Christian and Muslim believers. The notion of a God unaffected by space and time, eternal and unchanging, creating all ephemeral matter as an act of effortless sovereign coercion fit with the dominant metaphysics and physics of the Middle Ages and offered support in the early modern period for the eternity of Newtonian Law and the Cartesian dualism of timeless spirit and ephemeral matter.

Rashi notes, however, that the term *Bereishit* is a noun in the construct state with a finite verb: "When God began to create...." This reading understands the first phrase as awaiting completion with the third verse ("God said, 'Let there be light'"), with a parenthetical insertion ("the earth being unformed and void") describing the state of reality at the time God began the work of creation. God's creating, in Rashi's telling, is within time and space, as is God. Creation is an organizing of raucous potentiality, transforming chaos into cosmos.

Two and a half millennia of Western theology responding to Aristotle's physics have made it easy to forget that throughout the ancient Near Eastern world, including Israel, the point of creation is not the production of matter out of nothing, but rather the emergence of a stable community in a benevolent and life-sustaining order.[3]

That understanding of creation as a process within space-time, as a process of organizing the preexistent chaos, also commands a venerable biblical/rabbinic pedigree. One of the favorite rabbinic metaphors for God as creator is that of artist; "There is no rock [*tzur*] like our God" (1 Samuel 2:2) is transformed through a rabbinic pun: "There is no artist [*tzayar*] like our God" (Talmud, *Berakhot* 16b). Indeed, God is an artist of great enthusiasm: "The Rock is, as it were, an excellent artist. God is proud of God's world, and exclaims, 'See the creation that I created and the form that I constructed!'" (*Ecclesiastes Rabbah* 2; *Genesis Rabbah* 6:3). The greatness of God's creative artwork is twofold:

1. Creation is constantly unique and new: "How great is the Holy Blessing One! If a person mints a number of coins using the same die, each resembles the other. Yet the Majesty of Majesties, the Holy Blessing One, made each person in the die of Adam, and no one is like another" (Talmud, *Sanhedrin* 38a).

2. God's creations have the capacity to join God as co-creators, as artwork capable of itself creating new art: "A mortal may draw a picture, but the picture cannot draw a picture in turn. But when the Holy Blessing One draws a picture, God's picture makes other pictures. God made a woman, and the woman gives birth and produces others like herself" (*Tanchuma, Tazria* 3).

Artists are creators who use selected raw materials and fashion them into objects of great beauty and greater complexity through the infusion of their energy, intention, talent, and spirit. So too God's creation. Several rabbinic midrashim record the notion that God works with preexistent material to fashion the world and all that is in it:

From what were the heavens created? The Holy Blessing One took the garment of light that God wore and spread it as a cloak. (*Pirkei De-Rebbe Eliezer* 3)

How did the Holy Blessing One create the world? Rabbi Yochanan said, "God took two bundles, one of fire and one of snow, and beat them together, and from them earth was created." Rabbi Hanina said, "God took four bundles, representing the four directions of the compass, and one for above and one below." (*Bereishit Rabbah* 6:3)

Rabbi Hamma opened by quoting, "Take away the dross from the silver" (Proverbs 25:4). Rabbi Eliezer quoted Rabbi Jacob, "This is analogous to a bath full of water in which there were two beautiful bas-reliefs. As long as it was full of water, the bas-reliefs could not be seen. When the plug was pulled and the water flowed out of it, the bas-reliefs became visible. Similarly, as long as the world was *tohu va-vohu* [chaos], the heavens and earth could not be seen. When these were removed, the heavens and earth became visible. (*Sochar Tov* 22:4; *Bereishit Rabbah* 10:2)

Darkness and Deep

At the very moment God begins the process of creating, we encounter *tohu va-vohu*, the undomesticated chaos awaiting God's engagement, and a darkness (*choshekh*) permeates the surface of the deep (*tehom*) (Genesis 1:2). While most dominant theologies pay short shrift to this soothing darkness and the inviting pool, let us soak in its waters for a moment.[4] *Tohu va-vohu* is raw and chaotic—and we know that fractal beauty and order self-organize from the very heart of the chaotic. Chaos, an iterative nonlinear process, is neither rigid repetition nor pure random disorder; it offers rather a third way, an emergent, unpredictable becoming:

> The iteration of a fractal algorithm depicts not a predictable continuity of sameness, but a rhythm of repetition with a difference. Fractal "self-similarity" unfolds at different scales, like the whole enfolded in each part, the macrocosm in the microcosm.[5]

Linear formulas fail in the face of the very complexity, beauty, and fluidity of what emerges from the *tohu va-vohu*, the chaos. Too rich, too full of unpredictability and verve for objectified contemplation, what emerges from *tohu va-vohu* can only be lived, experienced, encountered, integrated into the patterns of becoming.

> Rabbi Huna quoted Bar Kappara: "Had the words not been written specifically, we would have been forbidden to say them: 'When God began to create the heavens and the earth....' Of what did God create them? 'The earth was *tohu va-vohu*.'" (*Bereishit Rabbah* 1:5)

The sheer promise of *tohu va-vohu*, its expectant potentiality, invites God's world-making attention—and ours—at every beginning, in every occasion.

Then there is the darkness (*choshekh*) on the face of the deep. To attend, patiently, with resolve and steadfastness, one must be free from glittering distraction. Darkness need not mean deprivation. Indeed, living in a world in which blackness still bears the toxins of racial degradation, poverty, and marginalization, it is particularly pressing to recognize the blessing of blackness—a shelter from white-knuckled terror that offers moments of creativity, that invites us to close our eyes in the security of the protective dark, in the quiet of the *choshekh* of repose and renewal. Rav Saadia notes, "Darkness is not a principle opposed to that of light, but merely the absence of light."[6] Sometimes the relentless glare of a hot white beam can rivet our attention to our wrinkles, inabilities, failures, and despair. In the forgiving shelter of the shadows, we can bask again in the embrace of promised new beginnings, ruddy good health and return, where there had only been fatigue and pallor. The sanctuary of darkness can provide a shielding safe space. Blackest night, the dark phase of our twenty-four-hour cycle around the sun, according to Rav Saadia, is also the time God gave us as a loving gift, for relaxation, for play, and for love: so we could "spend the night in relaxation, rest, sex, the practice of solitude, and similar pastimes."[7] When space-time first exploded into becoming, it was precisely the dark matter and dark energy that provided the potent causes luring the point of infinite potential to expand. That dark energy permeates everywhere and always, and it continues to bid the cosmos to swell. *Choshekh* is an expansive, pervasive, healing, powerful darkness—and it attracts the face of the deep even now.

Tehom is the whirling, primal waters out of which all life, all creativity emerge. Maternal in its nurturance, womb of fecundity and giving, of sheer abundance and sprawling becoming, *tehom* births worlds. Interestingly, *tehom* is treated like a female name: she "crouches below" (Genesis 49:25; Deuteronomy 33:13) and "roars loud" (Habakkuk 3:10), perhaps like a mother giving birth? Indeed, the Mesopotamian cognomen was Tiamat, a female personification of the primal ocean. Might we hear the muffled voice of the female, so often shunted aside and silenced? Shut her up, keep her home, yet here she comes, bubbling up again and again, turning her face to the vibrating flutters of creating. She will not be put aside; she cannot be domesticated or contained. So profound is our tehomophobia,[8] our fear of this chaotic, creative fertility, this female capacity to birth anew, that we leap over it in our most sacred story. Yet it is right there, even though it is the very locus where habit is sundered, where creation happens, always happens: "Your justice like the great deep [*tehom rabbah*]" (Psalm 36:7). It is in the chaos that novelty is birthed. It is in the openness and the potential that creativity advances. In the mutations are death but also evolution. It is there that renewal has a face—she beckons to us as the deep, *creatio ex profundis*.[9]

What we know about the Divine is that it returns again and again, to the darkness, to the deep. And it is precisely this tidal ebb and surge between chance and constraint, regularity and singularity, between novelty and conservation, continuation and change that drives the process of becoming. The deep, dark resurgence of what is possible births creation anew:

Who closed the sea behind doors

When it gushed forth out of the womb,

When I clothed it in clouds,

Swaddled it in dense clouds,

When I made breakers My limit for it,

And set up its bar and doors,

And said, "You may come so far and no farther;

Here your surging waves will stop"? (Job 38:8–11)

It is precisely here, at the face of *tehom*, that the breath of the Divine flutters, we are told, like a nesting dove over her fledgling chicks.[10] Concerned, protective, nurturing, urging her brood into flight, so too the *ruach* (breath, wind, spirit; Genesis 1:2) of God returns again and again to the edges of disorder and chaos, unsettling the norms, disrupting the habitual, comforting the afflicted and afflicting the comfortable,[11] cracking an opening for novelty to emerge. The Hebrew verb *merachefet* (Genesis 1:2), "to sweep or flutter," is "vibration, movement.... Motion, which is the essential element in change, originates with God's dynamic presence."[12] There are physicists who remind us that the components of matter are really vibrations, fluttering packets of energy shimmying the dance of becoming: "the microscopic landscape is suffused with tiny strings whose vibrational patterns orchestrate the evolution of the cosmos."[13] The divine vibrating resiliently invites chaos toward cosmos, organizing, constraining, enticing, luring. The work of creation is never-ending and never static. We are a part of its harvest, and we are, with the cosmos and the Divine, co-creators. The *ruach* continues to vibrate across the face of *tehom*, through us, in us, with us: *creatio continua*, continuous creating, across time.

10

Marking Time
The Jewish Calendar as a Prism on Creation

Eat and drink and celebrate before Me.
—Babylonian Talmud, *Chagigah* 10b

Time is, according to physics and Process Thought, not some abstract absolute, but rather the coordination of connected events. Time itself is a process, and a product of creation.

This insight, found in the Hebrew Bible and Rabbinics, and affirmed by almost every world culture as well as in contemporary science, seems jarring to most Western people, given our everyday perception of time as absolute. Uniquely in ancient Greek, Iranian, and Indian thought, in which *Chronos*, or *Zruuan*, or *Kāla* (time) has an objective and separate existence, and in Newtonian physics, that everyday sense of time as constant, objective, and absolute was the dominant way of conceptualizing chronology. But today we know that this sense of time as a power and a separate aspect of reality, or as something that flows on its own, is at best a useful metaphor and abstraction that does not correspond to any entity in objective reality:

> There is no underlying continuum on whose time everything is built; since, in other words, the idea of the time continuum only arises by a process of abstraction from higher levels of processes, then no sort of time has any privileged claim on reality.[1]

Unlike this Indo-European/Newtonian perception of absolute time, biblical and rabbinic thought, now vindicated by contemporary physics and expressed in Process philosophy, understands reality "as a series of discrete events and processes."[2] We now know that there is no such thing as absolute time; there is only time as perceived and experienced within specific relationships, from particular perspectives. No one time is truer than any other, and its reality, perception, and measurement correspond to the events being coordinated. In the words of Sacha Stern, professor of Rabbinic Judaism at University College London:

> It is perfectly possible to describe reality, including past and future events, without reference to a general, abstract dimension of time: instead, reality can be described in terms of an infinity of concrete, individual processes. In these "non-modern" societies, the key concept is thus not time but *process*. By "process" I simply mean a structured or meaningful sequence of events.[3]

Rethinking time as a series of events, as a linked set of processes, is another step in liberating our minds from the grip of dominant and often invisible Platonic assumptions, two of which are that creations are separate things and that time is objective and absolute.[4] Recognizing time as a process allows us to peel away this distortion, which became embedded in Jewish discourse during the medieval period, along with dominant notions of God as eternal, simple, and coercively all-powerful. The earlier understandings of Judaism, enshrined in the Torah, Mishnah, and Talmud, remain completely process-related. Reality was seen as a succession of objects and events, whereas the notions of time as an entity in itself, a human resource, a continuous flow, or a structure or dimension of the created world, were simply nonexistent. On close examination, this time-less, process-based approach to reality turns out to be eminently plausible.

Awareness, Gratitude, Devotion: A Calendar Spiral of Meaning

Girded with this ancient and renewed understanding, we recognize the priority of actual events, special moments, and our active role in their actualization. Shared moments of celebration and mourning, accomplishment and defeat forge solitary individuals into vibrant community. Since the earliest days of our history, we Jews have continuously constituted and renewed ourselves as a people through the commemoration of our shared joys and sorrows. The Jewish calendar helix, through its embodiment of Jewish theology and history, offers us a series of recurrent opportunities to perpetuate and encounter anew the values, beliefs, and history that have sustained us as a people, an *Am*. While there are certainly other prisms through which to appreciate the beauty and insights of Jewish life, our Sabbaths, holy days, festivals, memorials, and fast days offer a uniquely embodied experience of our faith, one cloaked in *mitzvot*, traditions, readings, and rituals and embedded in the distinctiveness of the unfolding seasons. A mindful engagement with our calendar offers lessons on how to live our lives with awareness, gratitude, and devotion.

The dominant understanding of time as timeless means that every point on a circle is identical to every other. In theory, this claim would be equally true for every day of the calendar—none possesses intrinsic meaning or distinction. The progression of days appears to be smooth and constant, with no inherent distinction between one day and the next. Yet nothing could be farther from a Jewish understanding of time as process nor from our subjective experience of time. We all know instinctively that in lived reality no two days are identical. Each has a texture and color provided by our moods, activities, challenges, and achievements. One of the functions of a calendar is to inscribe this lived experience on the passage of time, to recognize each day's distinctive identities. Calendars are, furthermore, a collective accounting of time, a communal endeavor to create and reaffirm meaning. They coordinate the relationship between events, illumining their relationship and what light they shine on each other's becoming.

Every people must grapple with how to mark the unending series of events that make up a life and collectively constitute history: through the observance of anniversaries, the celebration of agricultural cycles, the consecration of memorials, or the commemoration of mythic or historical events—the list goes on. The choices made are both reflective and definitional of who and what a particular community values. Americans, for example, celebrate the success of the American Revolution on Independence Day, self-sacrifice and service to the country on Memorial Day, and sense of indebtedness to their Creator and for the land's bounty on Thanksgiving Day. More recently, as the desire grew to enshrine tolerance and racial equality within the pantheon of public virtues, Martin Luther King's birthday was designated a national holiday.

The events that make up the Jewish calendar commemorate three distinct types of collective experience: natural events, historical events, and theological or spiritual themes. Let us examine each of these in turn to see the role it plays in structuring Jewish notions of time.

Natural Events

The most obvious units to mark the significant moments are the days, months, seasons, and solar years created by the cycles of the natural world. Even in our current era of electric lights and twenty-four-hour convenience stores, our pattern of activities is governed to a large extent by patterns of daylight and variations in day length, weather, and climate. How much more so was this the case for ancient Israel, an agricultural society whose work routines, living conditions, and food availability were governed by astronomical and meteorological forces beyond their awareness or control. It is unsurprising, then, that the most fundamental components of the Jewish calendar reflect the movement of celestial bodies.

While the Temple stood, the *kohanim* (priests) were given the simultaneously practical and sacred task of keeping communal calendars. Although they lacked the complex optics needed to fully comprehend the motion of the earth, moon, and other planetary bodies, they were able to construct a remarkably sophisticated luni-solar calendar. Lunar months, which were marked by the waxing and waning of the moon and lasted either twenty-nine or thirty days, depending on when the new moon was first sighted at the Temple in Jerusalem, were embedded in the solar year, which was timed relative to the recurrence of the agricultural seasons. Their calculations took into account the discrepancy of about eleven days between the length of the twelve lunar months and one solar year by intercalating seven lunar months over the course of a nineteen-year cycle, thus keeping the holidays and festivals in their proper seasons.

The relationship of the ancient Israelites to the heavenly orbs was not wholly unencumbered, however. Living in a cultural milieu in which the greater light rules the day and the lesser light governs the night (Genesis 1:16), the two great lights made by God were regarded by many of their neighbors as significant deities in their own right. The early proponents of monotheism, however, felt a need to domesticate the celebration of astronomical events and to ensure that the rituals that marked them were unambiguously oriented toward the worship of the Oneness from which the astral stars and planets emerged. Thus, while the Jewish calendar marks the new moon as a significant occasion, it prescribes that it be marked through the recitation of *Hallel*, a liturgy praising God as—among other attributes—the One who fashioned the sun, the moon, the stars, and other astral bodies. The reappearance of the moon is thus framed as a sign of God's steadfast love and creative bounty, rather than a marvel in its own right. Indeed, the ritual calendar further inscribes the arrival of the new month as an occasion for strengthening our relationship to the Divine by anticipating the new moon's arrival on the preceding Shabbat with a special prayer saying that the month ahead should be marked by love of Torah and the fear of sin. It further reinforces this message a few days after the new moon's arrival through the ritual of *Kiddush Levanah*, the recitation

of a psalm establishing God as the author of the natural order, noting that the sun, moon, and stars reliably respond to God's lure, and
implying that we should too.

Nested within the cycle of the lunar months and creating a yet
more proximate occasion for recognizing God's role in creation and
God's special relationship with the people Israel is the weekly celebration of Shabbat—the *only* calendrical unit that is not a reflection
of the motion of the sun, moon, or earth. Shabbat is not only the
capstone of the cycle of the days of the week, but it is also argu-
ably the pinnacle of Jewish holy days. In determining which greeting receives priority on those occasions when Shabbat and a holiday
coincide (*Shabbat shalom* or *Chag sameach*, i.e., "Happy festival"),
the Rabbis determined that the Shabbat greeting should come first.
Indeed, Shabbat takes precedence in every way; it is always the first
blessing offered, it is honored with the most numerous *aliyot* to the
Torah, and its laws take precedence over those specific to other holy
days. For example, we kindle the Chanukah lights before the candles
for Shabbat on Friday night and after the recitation of *Havdalah* on
Saturday. Far from being rendered prosaic by its frequency, Shabbat
is taken as a springboard for Jewish identity and observance. It is
credited by many of the sages, philosophers, mystics, and poets with
a redemptive role, instilling in the Jewish people a perpetual awareness of creation and the Exodus, while other commentators see this
day devoted to nonmaterial pursuits as an occasion for us to enlist as
God's partners in the work of liberation and justice.

Just as the designation of the weeks divided by Shabbatot
divides the moon's cycles into comprehensible periods of work
and rest, mirroring the work of creation itself, so the aggregation
of months into seasons marked by agricultural festivals plants in us
an awareness of the passage of larger relationships between seasons,
characterized by more profound changes both within us and around
us. The three pilgrimage festivals that anchor the Jewish calendar—
Passover, which by some reckonings begins the Jewish year and in
any case coincides with the spring harvest; Shavuot, fifty days later,

which marks the barley harvest in Israel; and Sukkot, the "festival of booths," which celebrates the completion of the fall harvest—impart a greater mindfulness of the bounteous, raw, undomesticated creation of which we are a part, inviting both awe and gratitude at God's wondrous world.

On the most encompassing level is the cycle of years that we group together to celebrate the periodic *Birkat Ha-Chammah*, the blessing of the sun. This ritual, mythically understood to be when the sun returns to the same position it was in at the moment of creation, is marked every twenty-eight years—the last occurrence was April 8, 2009; the next occurrence will fall on April 8, 2037. Like the monthly *Birkat Ha-Levanah*, the blessing of the new moon, this ritual takes place outdoors, focusing our attention on the astral bodies that make life on earth possible, moving our attention beyond the ebb of Jewish history and human spirit to the stars above and the cosmos itself as a repository of value, spirit, and oneness.

Historical Events

Connection with the rest of the natural world—or, more correctly, with God through creation—is but one of the bases on which the Jewish calendar is constructed. Another important function of the calendar is to both bind and define us as a people by linking us to our shared history and keeping it alive in our hearts. Many of the important events in our calendar serve primarily as markers of important events in Jewish history, including Chanukah, Tishah B'Av, Purim, Lag Ba-Omer, and, more recently, Yom Ha-Shoah and the national holidays that commemorate signal moments in the creation of the modern State of Israel. Each of these occasions not only reminds us of a specific experience in the long history of the Jewish people but also speaks to recurrent themes that continue to resonate in our inner and outer lives.

Indeed, so central is the creation of a collective pool of memories to the calendar's function that even occasions focused primarily on seasonal or ethical/spiritual concerns are also linked to a shared past, whether historical or mythical in origin. Thus Pesach, in addition to marking the arrival of spring, is identified with the Exodus from Egypt and, in particular, the crossing of the Red Sea. Shavuot is identified with receiving the Torah at Sinai. Even the Days of Awe, Rosh Ha-Shanah and Yom Kippur, the timing of which are only vaguely specified by the *Tanakh*, come to be fixed in our calendar through the celebration of the anniversary of creation.

The Jewish calendar, particularly the historical festivals, has evolved to reflect not only the progression of our history but also the progression of the ways we *think* about our history. This self-reflexivity is already evident in the early rabbinic debates about which historical occasions should be celebrated as events of national significance and on what terms. The Talmudic debate about the celebration of Chanukah (*"Mai Chanukah,"* in Talmud, *Shabbat* 21b), for example, reflects the profound discomfort of the rabbinic Sages with the elevation of a military victory to the status of a religious rite through the recitation of *Hallel*, a practice that was already widespread by the second century of the Common Era. Their discomfort was alleviated only when the martial victory was recast as an act of divine intervention, as evinced through the miracle of the oil. By contrast, outside of ultra-Orthodox communities there has been almost no debate about the recognition of the establishment of the State of Israel (Yom Ha-Atzma'ut) or the reunification of Jerusalem (Yom Yerushalayim) as historical events that nevertheless warranted the recitation of *Hallel*. The consensus on this matter reflects a widespread shift in Jewish consciousness, accepting human actors as themselves agents of divine providence.

This attunement to historical currents and willingness to incorporate and build upon the accrued insights of the ages is evident, too, in the manner in which the Jewish people mark even occasions of a predominantly seasonal or religious/spiritual nature. One has only to review the biblical passages describing the celebration of our most ancient rites to realize that none of our festivals or holy days—not even those mentioned in the *Tanakh* (Shabbat, Pesach,

Shavuot, Sukkot, Yom Kippur, and Rosh Chodesh)—has come to us in unchanged form. They were first and formatively fashioned in scripture, enhanced and expanded by the teachings of rabbinic Sages, and internalized and renewed in the writings of philosophers, kabbalists, and Hasidic masters in early modernity and our own time. Indeed, our celebration of our ritual helix differs even from the practices of our more recent forefathers and mothers in the shtetls of Europe, the *mellahs* of North Africa, or the *Yishuv* of pre-state Israel. And this is as it should be. As David HaLevi Segal, a seventeenth-century Polish commentator on the *Shulchan Arukh*, noted, "One is perpetually commanded to derive new teachings from the Torah ... for it is incumbent every moment to labor in the study of Torah and to innovate to the full extent of one's abilities."[5]

The practice of a Jewish life involves balancing a profound respect for tradition with recognition of the need to respond to ever-changing conditions and perceptions. Nowhere is this mix of conservation and innovation more evident than in the Pesach seder and, in particular, the Haggadah around which it is based. The Haggadah text and the rituals that it describes can be seen as a palimpsest, the layers of which can be peeled back to reveal a treasure trove of accumulated thought and ritual practice. This document, of which we are but the latest stewards, reflects more than two thousand years of evolving insights into the Exodus story and its motifs. Yet far from becoming ossified through the accretion of so much collective wisdom, the Haggadah has remained a supple, living text, which even in our own day is viewed as a "work in progress," a still-wet canvas to which we are invited to add our own narratives, customs, and interpretations. As Rabbi Abraham ibn Ezra (twelfth century) stated with respect to the Sages of yore, and as we, as contemporary Jews, hold with respect to those involved in the study and practice of Torah in every generation, "By utilizing their great wisdom and casuistic powers, the Sages were able to derive new meanings from biblical texts."[6]

That said, embedded in Judaism is a deep-seated respect for the contributions of those who have come before us and a firm insistence that our religious life develop as a continuous evolution, rather than as a jarring revolution or break with the past. As the great twentieth-century scholar of Jewish mysticism Gershom Scholem reminds us, "We must arouse in the next generation a sense of understanding and of general identification with the great heritage of the generations."[7] Thus, our observance of the festivals is grounded in *halakhah* (legal precedent) and *minhag* (customary practice or tradition), which together constitute an instruction manual as to how to mark events and make them holy, whether through reciting special liturgy, restructuring daily activities, consuming or abstaining from certain foods, participating in charitable giving, or performing other distinctive rites.

Theological or Spiritual Themes

No event in the Jewish calendar, however prosaic its origins, lacks a theological and spiritual underpinning. The insertion of practices of holiness and occasions for drawing closer to God into the fabric of our daily lives is a persistent priority of the Jewish calendar and, indeed, of Jewish life. That said, there are certain moments in the Jewish year when sacred themes figure more prominently than others.

Shining supreme among the holy days, Shabbat recalls and reenacts God's primal, sovereign rest. On this day, the labors of premodern agriculture specify how we define labor and therefore the tasks we must avoid. On Shabbat, we explicitly rest in identification with the Creator and in remembrance of the acts of creation, and then with the arrival of Saturday evening, we resume the ongoing work of creation as God's partners. The Sabbath invites us to celebrate our liberation from slavery through affirmative acts of Jewish belonging and celebration—festive meals, joyous worship, companionship, relaxation, and rest—all of which were precluded for our enslaved ancestors.

The year can, on a deeper level, provide a circle, which we round with each passing month. The two pivots of the year are the cluster of the *Yamim Nora'im*, Days of Awe (the month of Elul, Selichot,

Rosh Ha-Shanah, *Aseret Yemei Teshuvah* [Ten Days of Repentance], Yom Kippur), which are the most introspective and the least connected to a historical event of any season of the year, and, at the opposite side of the calendar, Purim and Pesach (Passover), which are the most communal and public commemorations of the year. As we move from the introspective and personal time of the Days of Awe, we transition through Sukkot and Chanukah, which offer a blend of the personal and the communal, the introspective and the historical, on our way to Pesach. And after Pesach concludes, we cycle through the *Sefirat Ha-Omer* (counting of the barley grain), Shavuot, and Tishah B'Av on our way back from the public toward the introspective. The Jewish year marks a constant swinging from one pole to the other.

As we spiral between the poles of the year, with an introspective focus at the Days of Awe and a communal emphasis for Passover and Shavuot, we affirm that each occasion in the Jewish year expresses profound ethical responsibilities embedded in the Torah and our rabbinic sources for how we treat our fellow human beings, other living things, and creation as a whole. Each also resonates with opportunities to deepen our inner life and the spiritual discipline that a path of holiness makes possible. Passover, for example, bids us to renew our commitment to our own liberation—political, communal, and spiritual—and to work all the more resolutely for freedom and justice for all. Shavuot asks us to listen for the divine *kol demamah dakah*, the still, small voice, to discern God's invitation to live a life of relationship, connection, and joy. Sukkot bids us to reflect on the false security of our solid structures and to embrace the resilient fragility of sheltering love—God's and each other's. Chanukah offers the chance to renew our commitment to Jewish independence and pride, to light a candle in the darkness, and Purim helps us to laugh at our enemies and at our own shortcomings.

For a person who links his or her life to the rhythms of Jewish life—personal, communal, and historical—the cycles of the Jewish calendar offer ever new ways to reconnect and reaffirm. Each new day is no mere repetition of an eternal past. Instead, the Jew finds eternity nestled within each new event, as the richness of the seasons provide a regular reminder of our covenantal past, a present to hallow with acts of empathy, holiness, and justice, and a future resonant with hope and joy.

Part IV
CREATION ETHICS

God loves what is right and just,
the earth is full of God's love.
By the word of the Holy One the heavens were made,
by the breath of God's mouth, all their host.
—Psalm 33:5–6

In part 4, we move from worldview and ideas to their implications in behavior. That religious litmus test, certainly for Judaism, places the center of gravity in ethical behavior. Convictions that matter emerge in action, specifically in how we treat each other and the rest of creation.

Chapter 11 takes the values that emerge from the scientific telling of beginnings and the scriptural enactment in Genesis and in Rabbinics. Those two sources pool together to shape a creation ethics that implements belonging and gratitude in the pattern of responsibility and stewardship.

Chapter 12 applies those values of belonging and gratitude into an ethical stance of stewardship, a biblical, values-based relationship to the rest of creation. As a steward, humanity assumes the role of caretaker for the vitality of the biosphere. Chapter 13 continues that discussion by moving beyond caretaker, looking at our role in fostering the raucous diversity that allows all living things to thrive, regardless of their utility for one species in particular. Both chapters present numerous instances in which Jewish narrative and law implement these responsibilities.

Finally, looking at the way that all living things are born and must die, chapter 14 reflects on what it means to die in such a way as to give back to the living system from which we emerge and to which we return, so that our lives and deaths each contribute to life as a whole.

Life as Good, Earth as Home

The conception of God as Creator, which we established, implies the attributes of Life, Power, and Wisdom.[1]
—Rav Saadia Gaon, *Emunot Ve-De'ot* 2:4

Ruach *(spirited energy) vibrates as deeds of novelty, relationship, and* increasing complexity, and it is in this integrated action that our two previously divergent paths converge: creation as process revealed through the natural sciences *and* creation as process known through the revelation of the stories and laws of scripture.[2]

Both paths converge at the *dayenu* point, gratitude—that explosive, fructifying, singularity-generating, and resilient attitude of thankfulness that finds expression in myriad deeds of loving-kindness. Gratitude is an emotion, a response, and also a virtue—an ongoing, cultivated trait of character that is valued as good. One central commitment of human becoming involves translating gratitude from an upwelling spontaneous feeling—an exclaimed "Halleluyah!"—into the steady balancing work of character formation:

> It behooves a person to self-accustom to the practice of good
> deeds until the virtue is acquired corresponding to those good
> deeds; and, furthermore, to abstain from evil deeds so that

one may eradicate the vices that may have taken root. Let one not suppose that one's characteristics have reached such a state that they are no longer subject to change, for any one of them may be altered from the good to the bad and vice versa; and, moreover, all in accordance with his own free will.[3]

More than just an internal middle way (*derekh ha-beinoni*), gratitude also inspires engagement with others—taking risk, sharing pain, and extending help. How we embrace other human becomings, other natural events, overbrims our attention from the emotional, intuitive, cognitive realm of thought to the relating and doing of ethics and morality. What we are inspired to do with our relating, with the ontological unity of all becoming, with our prehension of every other natural event resonating with and in us, and our dawning sense of our own belonging calling us to act responsibly, lovingly, toward the creation of which we are a part, moves us from engaged contemplation to thoughtful action.

Creation Ethics: Belonging and Gratitude

Ethics comes to us and emerges from us in two broad, intersecting swaths—from the process of creation and inscribed in our interpretations of revelation. The latter shape our understanding of ourselves, our place in the world, and our responsibilities in the language of the narratives and norms of specific cultures, in our case the vast edifice of *aggadah* and *halakhah*. There is a revelation ethic of creation too. But for the present, in this volume, it is the ethics we process from creation that invites our primary attention. Creation ethics is the implementation of belonging and gratitude.

A creation ethics begins with the relatedness of all living things, the dynamic interactivity of the biosphere with the rest of creation, our profound community of all that is. The science of such belonging is ecology, and the realm of its ethical and political implementation is environmentalism. A creation ethic reflects a cosmic perspective. As we noted with regard to evolution and creation:

- We learn from both narratives.
- All is connected to all.
- We are related each individually to the totality of creation.
- All creation is related to all of its parts.

These insights combine to affirm an ethics of belonging and an interlocking set of consequences. Every response or choice of any component of the system will have an effect on every other natural event of the system, and that impact, for conscious creatures such as human beings, creates responsibility. Awareness that what we do and the choices we make have an influence on the rest of the biosphere spares us from occupying the center of our own concerns. Awareness of cosmic community prevents us from perpetuating an outmoded rhetoric as though the world were intentionally designed to culminate in homo sapiens, as though we were self-evidently the purpose and the capstone of all being. Maimonides reproves those who presume that humans represent the pinnacle of creation:

> It should not be believed that all the beings exist for the sake of the existence of humanity. On the contrary, all the other beings too have been intended for their own sakes and not for the sake of something else.[4]

All creation is a pageant of diversity and unity, embodied in specific natural entities. The same recycled stardust constitutes us all, and we remain energized by the power unleashed by the big bang. With such awareness, the very first value a creation ethic expresses is a reverence for all living things, a shared solidarity with the family of life, and a commitment to maintain diversity, not merely as a tool for human betterment—although it is that—but as an end in itself, a model of inclusion among humans and across species.

The Path of Stewardship
Humanity's Relationship toward the Earth

> Bountiful is the Place of the World [God] who
> handed the world over to guardians.
> —Talmud, *Avodah Zarah* 40b

Across human history, three general ways of understanding the proper contours of humanity's relationship to the earth have emerged:

1. As a machine to be used and discarded at will

2. As a living organism of superior worth to any of its components (for example, humanity)

3. Somewhere in the middle, subject to the kind of human use that is constrained by larger ethical considerations[1]

All three viewpoints can claim an ancient and venerable pedigree within Western civilization, and each of the three are quite incompatible. We live in an age in which the choices that our societies make about how we use the earth's resources, care for the diversity of living species, tend to delicate and endangered bioregions, and respond to our own exploding population—underlying assumptions about what is proper in our treatment of the planet—can have serious and possibly life-threatening implications for our own survival and the well-being of other living things. It is therefore time, once again, to consider what we owe our earth and what we may legitimately expect from it.

One view, rooted in some Stoic thinkers, understands the earth as a machine to be used for human pleasure and asserts that irrational creatures lack rights. According to this viewpoint, the earth is nothing more than the dirt on which we walk, and its nonhuman residents are unthinking, mobile sources of protein, entertainment, or danger. That all was made for the sake of humankind influenced certain early Christian thinkers, notably Origen (third-century Egyptian theologian), Thomas Aquinas (thirteenth-century Italian friar and theologian), and John Calvin (sixteenth-century French theologian). In the early modern period, this mechanistic understanding of the world as a bag of tools ready for any human purpose reached its clearest expression, particularly in the words of French philosopher René Descartes, who sought to find

> a practical philosophy by means of which, knowing the force and the action of fire, water, air, the stars, heavens, and all other bodies which environ us, as distinctly as we know the different crafts of our artisans, we can in the same way employ them in all those uses to which they are adapted, and thus render ourselves the masters and possessors of nature.[2]

For Descartes, there was a wall of separation between humanity, on the one hand, and all other creatures and objects on the other. Consistent with his own premises, he thus held that animals were automata and that "there can be no suspicion of crime when [people] eat or kill animals."[3]

The Stoics, Descartes, and his followers were not entirely wrong. Humanity is indeed different from other living things in significant ways—in our ability to conceptualize, to communicate across generations, to engage in introspection, and to manipulate tools and technology, to name a few distinguishing traits. How our species acts does have a disproportionate influence on the world around us. Our willingness to see beyond what merely is and to strive for what might yet be, using an empirical scientific method, has resulted in better and healthier lives for millions of people. Few of us would surrender the benefits of technology and culture to return to premodern life. A relationship to the earth as something to be used to heighten human pleasure is part of what has allowed us to fashion comfortable and civilized life.

Yet there are clear dangers to elevating this functional approach to a totalized mechanistic viewpoint. Our interventions in the world can have intended and beneficial consequences but can often unleash unintended and disastrous consequences, even if we look only at the impact of those actions on people. Loss of farmland across North America is but one example of our sovereignty over nature exacting a frightening and unanticipated cost. As frightening as the results of our interventions may be, we are diminished when we reduce our horizons to cost-benefit considerations alone. As the twentieth-century theologian Rabbi Abraham Joshua Heschel noted:

> Human beings have indeed become primarily tool-making animals, and the world is now a gigantic tool box for the satisfaction of their needs.... Nature as a tool box is a world that does not point beyond itself. It is when nature is sensed as mystery and grandeur that it calls upon us to look beyond it. The awareness of grandeur and the sublime is all but gone from the modern mind. The sense of the sublime—the sign of inward greatness of the human soul and something which is potentially given to all—is now a rare gift. Yet without it, the world becomes flat and the soul a vacuum.[4]

Is the world not impoverished when a species disappears? Is a beautiful glen or a majestic mountain not something of intrinsic worth, something to be cherished and protected? We humans have a limited notion of self-interest, and we endanger our own children and grandchildren for the sake of our short-term desires. Seeing the earth as a big bag of tools encourages rapacity and endangers human survival and the balance of life on earth. The time has long passed when this was an acceptable way to construe our role in the world.

Gaia: The Earth as an Organism

A second, corrective approach to human relations to the rest of reality asserts that the earth constitutes a living entity, often referred to as Gaia.[5] This personification of the earth, sometimes intended as metaphor and sometimes quite literally as a real individual, asserts that the earth functions as an organism to maintain its own balance. As humanity grows and claims more and more of the earth's resources, the earth will act—rightfully—to control this threat to its own functioning, just as a cell acts to expel a source of danger. All living things together form a coherent organism. Humanity, in this view, threatens the biosphere and will be removed, by nature, in a surgical strike to defend itself.

While there were certainly ancient civilizations that perceived the earth as a divinity, often a goddess, and that goddess was often seen as hostile to human interests and security, this philosophical approach that recognizes humans as but one small part of the web of nature, properly curtailed by the general good of the biosphere, is a modern innovation with much to commend it: we are indeed part of the physical universe. Not having chosen to be born, we did not fashion this world, and the cosmos makes felt its own limits and priorities all the time. To disregard our membership in—and dependence on—the totality of living things courts disaster. Yet there is something ironic to the view that we are merely subservient to Gaia, that nature is morally superior to the needs of humanity. The irony becomes especially clear when we stop to ponder just how unnatural such a viewpoint is: What other species sublimates its own desires for the common good of the biosphere? What other living creature denies its own pleasure in order to, as naturalist Aldo Leopold put it, learn "to think like a mountain"?[6] To be truly natural would be to follow our impulses and do as we please. The advocates of the Gaia position are, intellectually, the least natural of the three competing viewpoints.

That unnatural stance fails for another reason as well: only people can articulate what is "good" for the earth, and that assertion must always reflect the viewpoint of some particular perspective. Who can say whether or not the earth is better off with living things or without? With mammals dominant, rather than roaches?[7] Perhaps the earth is indifferent or would even like an extra strip mall? Only people argue about such things and seem to express strong preferences. The earth just keeps circling the sun. Imputing preferences to geological or astronomical entities confuses "ought" and "is" in a way that makes for a tyranny of what currently exists, imposing the current momentary balance as a rigid fixture for all time. Unnatural and unreasonable, such an approach also fails in that it has little possibility of appealing to the vast majority of human beings whose choices will fashion our collective response to the environmental crisis that threatens our health and security. While the general acceptance of the Gaia hypothesis might curtail human greed and shortsightedness, it has little chance of gaining that assent. And its many flaws—not least its lack of compassion for human suffering—would raise serious problems of their own, were it ever adopted. This second path, powerful as metaphor, is not a feasible choice either.

"To Till and to Tend": Stewardship

There is one remaining way to understand our relationship to the earth. Its pedigree is as ancient as the Hebrew Bible and as current as most conservation organizations. Because it is so embedded in our culture, because it appears so reasonable to so many, it stands the greatest chance of receiving an attentive hearing from the vast numbers needed to make real environmental change. That middle path is stewardship, the notion that humanity is the caretaker of the earth and of all living things.[8] This approach is made clear in the very heart of the Torah: "The land is Mine; you are but strangers resident with Me. Throughout the land that you hold, you must provide for the redemption of the land" (Leviticus 25:23–24).

Rooted in a religious view of the world, stewardship asserts that the purpose of all creation, humanity included, is to sing God's praises through deeds of goodness, through establishing a just and righteous society, by cultivating gratitude to our Creator for the marvel of being alive. That task does not fall just on humanity; as the psalmist reminds us, "the heavens declare the glory of God" (Psalm 19:2). The purpose of creation, then, is not humankind nor are we creation's pinnacle—recall that the Sabbath day is created after humanity. We exist to make the world sacred and decent.

As part of creation, we also manifest distinct abilities that other parts of creation do not. "What is humanity that You have been mindful of them ... You have made them little less than divine" (Psalm 8:5–6). Our added gifts—consciousness, speech, law—are intended to assist us in our task of serving as God's agents in the world. The biblical view of our role in relation to the rest of creation is that we "till and tend" the world on God's behalf, for the sake of God's majesty.

This ideal of stewardship integrates important components of the two views previously mentioned. It shares with the mechanists the belief that human well-being is the proper vantage point from which to judge morality, but it broadens that sense of well-being to a solidarity with all of creation and a desire to avoid unnecessary suffering for all living things. It shares with the Gaiaists a sense that holiness and wholeness emerge from the wonder and the miracle of God's world, but it refuses to deify any part of creation, humanity included. Existence is what is; morality, what ought to be. Humanity's role is to bridge that gap in the direction of what ought to be, to work toward the repair of the world as a healing, holy place.

Stewardship sees humanity legitimately using the bounty of the world for moral ends, as God's agents. We are God's hands in the world, to care, to improve, and to love creation. But the world is not, ultimately, ours to abuse. We tend it in God's name and therefore must extend God's tender mercies to creation else we violate our charge. Note, then, that the steward is at once someone who acts on behalf of all nature, taking instruction and direction from a sense of morality and reverence that embodies a cosmic perspective. Yet the steward is also profoundly and gratefully a particular aspect of creation; it is that very particularity that allows us to act in the world on God's behalf, and on creation's behalf. A little lower than the angels, sharing the finitude of all flesh-and-blood, we are precisely located to know both world and holiness and to bridge those two perspectives in a single whole.

Dominion Is Not Domination

Our task, then, is to act responsibly, to assure that the beauty and majesty of the world not be lessened by our deeds, to see that all of God's creatures can know, at whatever level, the goodness of creation, to make visible the unity of God through the solidarity of all created things, and to justify the assertion that humanity faithfully reflects God's image by our unique responsibility for caring for God's world.

An old rabbinic legend records that God escorted the first human being through the Garden of Eden. After the tour, God said, "Look at My works! See how beautiful they are—how excellent! For your sake I created them all. See to it that you do not spoil and destroy My world; for if you do, there will be no one else to repair it" (*Ecclesiastes Rabbah* 7:13). Our distinction as people, our very claim to dominion in the world, rests on our ability to distinguish good from evil, to restrain our desires, to consider the whole and the holy. As economic theorist Jeremy Rifkin reminds us, "We have misread our mandate. We believed that to have dominion meant to exert power, to control, to dominate."[9] Liberated from a theology of a God whose power is coercive and static, we can open a path for participatory, relational engagement with the rest of creation.

Elements of a Jewish Environmental Ethics

What, then, are the principal areas of Jewish environmental concern, arenas in which we are called to exercise responsible stewardship for all the denizens of our shared planet?

- *Bal Tashchit*: This commandment requires humanity to refrain from waste or from wanton destruction. While the Torah's pro-hibition is directed specifically against destroying sources of food, rabbinic tradition expands this edict to preclude all wasteful destruction. If, as the psalmist sings, "the earth is the Holy One's" (Psalm 24:1), then it is not our property to dispose of. Rather, we must cherish its bounty and resourcefulness as ours to be enjoyed and then returned. In truth, everything we use we borrow; and we can return what we have used either in a form that it can be easily reintegrated into the natural order or in a way that will impede the living system that is our world. The *mitzvah* of *bal tashchit* is one that impels us to attend to life and the world as a single system, in which we are increasingly powerful—hence dangerous—participants. *Bal tashchit* is God's warning to be careful and to tread lightly.

- *Tza'ar Ba'alei Chayim:* This commandment requires humanity to show compassion to all other forms of life. Midway between animal rights and human wrongs, it affirms the distinct sanctity of human life by insisting that we may not treat animals the way they treat each other. Precisely because we are "little less divine" than the angels (Psalm 8:6) we must act toward nonhuman animals in a way consistent with moral concerns, not simply to indulge our own desires or pleasures. *Tza'ar ba'alei chayim* implies a consciousness of the needless way animals suffer at the hands of human beings and an insistence that humans may take animals' lives only when it is necessary for human survival. *Tza'ar ba'alei chayim* requires shifting our consumption away from an excessive ingestion of animal flesh, the ostentatious display of animal hair and skins as human adornment, and the mutilation or torture of terrified, tormented animals for our own amusement.

- *Shabbaton* and *Yovel:* Biblical Israel understood that the earth possesses the necessary tools for its own regeneration and fertility and that humanity benefits from respecting that natural cycle of rest and rebirth. Consequently, the Torah records a mandate to allow the earth to rest uncultivated every seven years (*Shabbaton*, the Sabbatical year) and for that pattern of seven times seven years to culminate in the *Yovel*, the Jubilee year, during which the earth is to lie fallow. Indeed, even Shabbat, Israel's great gift to the world, is, in part, the ritualized acknowledgment that the earth is only ours to use as caretakers and tenants. That respect for our tenancy on a planet not our own possession also has immediate implications for how people treat each other and the land. Thus the Israelite farmer is enjoined not to re-harvest a field: all overlooked produce becomes the property of the poor. So too, tithing for the priests, the Levites, and the poor is—remarkably—categorized within ancient Israel's legislation for living in harmony with the land.

If all creatures are interconnected, then all is one. If economic justice requires political freedom, which in turn requires a blend of adequate sustenance, secure shelter, sustainable development, limiting our drive for consumer goods, and a tended environment, then, indeed, each is a part of all.[10] Then, indeed, God's oneness is not just a theological stance but a clarion call for involvement, engagement, and change. On the day that we attend to all these concerns, on the day that we make the earth our home and all creatures our family, then truly, in the words of the prophet Zechariah, "God shall be one, and God's name shall be one" (Zechariah 14:9).

Beyond Stewardship
A Partnership Celebrating Biodiversity

> How diverse are the works of the
> Holy Blessing One!
> —*Pesikta Rabbati, Piska* 15

"Biodiversity" signifies the variety of living things on earth, the array of species, both plant and animal, and the genetic variation within each species. Life reveals a marvelous propensity to increase its diversity with the passage of time. From an anthropocentric perspective, the term also denotes the way living things constitute a resource base for humanity. This diversity is responsible for a range of global functions necessary for human survival, such as the biochemical flows of energy (through photosynthesis), water, carbon, nitrogen, and phosphorus, as well as providing a pool of genetic resources. Biodiversity offers other less utilitarian benefits as well—aesthetic (the beauty of so many living forms and their interactions), intellectual (constituting a library of information and relationships), and social (a sense of community across the biosphere).

Life's diversity conveys important scientific, aesthetic, and utilitarian benefits. Humanity as a species is finally becoming aware of the complex ways in which living things interact to maintain the delicate balance that sustains life itself. Even a little rupture in that complex interaction can create unforeseen and harmful consequences elsewhere in the system, just as breaking one strand of a spider's web can create chaos at the far end of its handiwork.

In the past, human presence and action may have threatened the biology of particular locales, but we lacked the power and the numbers to constitute a threat to the health of the environment worldwide. Our intervention was sufficiently limited that the survival of most species did not depend on our actions. Humankind now has the capacity to alter the environment on a global scale; we have made ourselves a global force of nature. Able to mold and disrupt the entire biosphere, we nonetheless remain subject to the vagaries of the world around us. The consequences of human action now constrain and threaten human survival. Our assault on the ozone layer, tropical coral reefs, and the Amazonian rainforest are but a few prominent examples. Hence, we are simultaneously actors and objects of our own newfound and little-comprehended powers. We have taken ourselves hostage, and our release depends on our ability to preserve the fragile ecological balance that rests on the foundation of biodiversity.

Shutafut: Partnership in Diversity

Biodiversity is, however, not only a matter of scientific, aesthetic, and political concern. Diversity is a matter of pressing Jewish concern. Since Judaism understands nature as God's ongoing creation, cultivating marvel at the teeming abundance of life and the diverse array of living things is intrinsic to our religious experience.[1] Indeed, the experience of holiness through nature has inspired the world's religious traditions.[2] Each faith tradition has responded to the wonder of the world in its own ways; in Judaism, one fetching response, suggested in the previous chapter, has been to see humanity as God's partner (*shutaf*) in creation. This partnership (*shutafut*) is a form of stewardship *and* an expression of covenant, both of which are concretized in Torah and subsequent Jewish tradition. Stewardship emerges—as we have seen—from the texts of Genesis, emphasizing humanity's unique responsibility to guard and care for creation. We are God's stewards, responsible to "guard and tend" (Genesis 2:15) creation. As the psalmist reminds us, "The heavens belong to God, but the earth was given to humanity" (Psalm 115:16). Our special obligation is to ensure the continuing viability of creation, to maintain the earth's bounteous ability to nurture life. Since Judaism recognizes humanity as God's stewards, our commitment to sustain diversity is nothing short of a religious mandate, a *mitzvah*.

Humanity: A Part of Creation, Yet Distinct Nonetheless

Yet our role as steward is nothing *more* than a *mitzvah* either; we are not obligated to negate our own interests or necessitated to harm ourselves for the benefit of other living creatures. After all, we have as much right as any other creatures to pursue our own benefit. Indeed, biblical/rabbinic tradition would go beyond that minimal standard to insist that human beings are unique among all created things, since we alone are made in God's image. Sole possessors of consciousness and language, people are privileged to reflect the sacred within the mundane and to translate the worldly into the spiritual. Judaism creates a fruitful tension by insisting that people are both a part of creation and in some characteristics distinct within it; we are little higher than the beasts, and "little less divine" than the angels (Psalm 8:6). As unique creatures within creation, we can legitimately use the rest of creation to meet our needs as a species (just as do all the other animals). Reflecting God's image in the world, however, we must also consider how well we are managing the world on behalf of its Creator.[3]

Some have criticized those same biblical texts for what appears to be anthropocentrism—seeing our role not only as responsibility to care for the whole of creation but also dominion as the assertion of mastery, coercion, and self-gratification.[4] That some religious people have also read the Bible (Hebrew and Greek) through this lens, particularly in the early modern and industrial periods, has led to the conscription of religious rhetoric to sanction reliance on technology and acquisition as the defining measurement of a well-lived life and the sufficient tools to solve all human dilemmas. We live in the age in which that bankrupt ideology of conquest and exploitation now threatens human survival as well as the biosphere's capacity to continue to thrive. As we struggle to free ourselves from this Procrustean straitjacket, we can also liberate the hijacked import of the biblical message. Stewardship, in biblical expectation, did indeed elevate humanity as the responsible agent for caring for creation as a whole—people are uniquely fashioned, according to the Torah, "in God's image" (Genesis 1:27). That anthropocentrism may yet need further correction, but it is a far cry from industrial exploitation and its deliberate cultivation of human narcissism, disdain for the rest of creation, and casual self-destruction. Stewardship, properly understood, is an invitation to partnership pertaining not only to Jews but also to all humans. That universalism is clear from the following midrash:

> It has been taught: When the child is formed in its mother's womb, there are three partners concerned with it: the Holy Blessing One, the father, and the mother. (*Ecclesiastes Rabbah* 5:12)

While the midrash goes on to specify the contributions of each of the three partners, our focus rests on the recognition of the interdependence of all three agents—the Divine working in, with, and through us. The midrash also directs our attention toward our human contribution, which is no less active, significant, and real. What we humans do and how we do it have a lasting impact on the rest of creation. In that sense, our dominion is no mere theological projection; it is a biological and geological factor of great significance. As individuals, the impacts of our choices and actions empower and constrain the choices and actions of those whose lives interact with our own as well as the balance and interaction of the lithosphere, hydrosphere, and atmosphere. As communities and as a species, humanity's collective choices and actions exercise significant environmental impact globally.

Rabbinic traditions coalesce around two concrete modes of human partnership with the Divine: the realm of intentions and words, and the realm of relationships and right actions. The paradigm for impactful speech is prayer, and here the Rabbis focus on two classical prayers:

> Raba—others attribute it to Rabbi Joshua ben Levi—said: Even an individual who prays on the eve of the Sabbath must recite, "The heaven and the earth were finished" (Genesis 2:1); for Rabbi Hamnuna said: One who prays on the eve of the Sabbath and recites "the heaven and the earth were finished," scripture considers that person a partner with the Holy Blessing One in creation, for it is said, *Va-yekhullu* [and they were finished]; read not *va-yekhullu* but *va-yekhallu* [and they finished]. (Talmud, *Shabbat* 119b)

How intriguing that Shabbat, considered a sign both of creation and of the Exodus from slavery, is at the epicenter of this partnership with God. As Jews enter into the Sabbath—visible demonstration of God's love for the people of Israel—we accept our role as God's partners through the recitation of the biblical verses celebrating the culmination of the creation story. By reciting the story we make ourselves participants in the ongoing reality of creation itself. Retelling the tale empathically, reading ourselves into the biblical telling, is how we join with the Divine in the ongoing work of creation.

The second prayer that highlights this partnership is the *Kaddish*, ancient liturgy recited at the house of study and later adapted for recitation at burials and memorial services:

> This is what the Sages say: All who answer "Amen, may God's great name ..." with all their strength are partners with the Holy Blessing One in the work of creation and even receive the Torah at Mount Sinai."[5]

Just as we saw in the previous midrash, creation and Exodus/Sinai are linked through our active recitation of story and prayer. In this case, responding to the *Kaddish*, the great doxology of ancient Judaism, enlists the participant as a partner with God in the work of creation. Not only that, but such a recitation also creates anew the act of giving and receiving Torah.

In addition to the mode of intentions and words, the second cluster of modes for partnership centers around relationship and right action:

> Every judge who judges with complete fairness even for a single hour, scripture credits as though that judge had become a partner to the Holy Blessing One in the work of creation. [For] here it is written, "The people stood about Moses from the morning into the evening" (Exodus 18:13); while elsewhere it is written, "There was morning, and there was evening, one day" (Genesis 1:5). (Talmud, *Shabbat* 10a)

Here the event that creates a vibrant partnership between human and the Divine is the administration of justice, doing the work of making community possible. Other versions of this same midrash speak of judging truly—presumably of applying Torah to enhance and contribute to human lives and relationships.

As Jews, we are the heirs to an ancient heritage through which we can reflect on our place in the world and our responsibilities to God, humanity, and creation. While the issue of biodiversity per se reflects a modern environmental concern, both in the realm of Jewish legend and in Jewish law, sages across the millennia have expressed their marvel at the variety of living things and a concern for the integrity of creation. As the psalmist reminds us, "How great are Your works, Holy One!" (Psalm 92:6).

While Judaism certainly allows people to use the resources of the world to sustain human development and well-being, permitting taking animals' lives for human nutrition and health and harvesting plants for human civilization, the Jewish balancing act—established from the beginning—is to "guard and to tend" (Genesis 2:15) the garden in which we live, but which we do not own. This "tending" is often understood in terms of a benevolent, expansive self-interest. As Process theologian John Cobb reminds us:

> The anthropocentric bias of Western ethics is reflected in the sorts of justification which are provided as standard for the preservation of the natural environment. Godfrey-Smith[6] lists four such arguments, which he calls the silo argument (for maintaining a stockpile of useful organisms), the laboratory argument (for scientific enquiry), the gymnasium argument (for leisure) and the cathedral argument (for aesthetic pleasure). All are arguments to look after nature because nature looks after us.[7]

What we seek is the next step, to advance the stewardship model—the first pillar of partnership (*shutafut*)—beyond enlightened self-interest to cultivate a recognition of all creation, humans and others, as agents with standing, as distinct and unique, and as valuable in their own right. To make this move, we draw upon the second pillar of partnership, that of covenant. That covenant draws from the past, objectively and eternally in the divine mind, and opens to a liberating future of community and interdependence among all living creatures. The covenant is of the past:

> "When the bow is in the clouds, I will see it and remember the everlasting covenant between God and all living creatures, all flesh that is on earth. That," God said to Noah, "shall be the sign of the covenant that I have established between Me and all flesh that is on earth." (Genesis 9:16–17)

The covenant is from the future:

> In that day, I will make a covenant for them with the beasts of the field, the birds of the air, and the creeping things of the ground; I will also banish bow, sword, and war from the land. Thus I will let them lie down in safety. (Hosea 2:20)

All living things, by virtue of their participation in the web of life, have instrumental value for other living things—their kin, their progeny, their community, their prey, and their predators, to name a few. Yet those same living things also possess intrinsic worth—actual occasions, agents actively affirming their own integrity, opportunities for the working of the Divine throughout creation. I mean to designate such a recognition with the notion of *shutafut*, of partnership as a particular kind of stewardship—one that recognizes the unique human consciousness and impact, hence responsibility toward all of creation, while at the same time moving past notions of human supremacy and self-interest toward a reverent community of living things. One of the world's foremost Christian environmental ethicists, Larry L. Rasmussen, speaks of "a kind of 'holy democracy' of all creatures great and small" and says that "other creatures are co-siblings of creation in the drama of a shared life."[8] In the words of the psalmist, "I praise You, for I am awesomely, wondrously made; Your work is wonderful; I know it very well" (Psalm 139:14).

Creation: Different Is Good

Recognizing, celebrating, and protecting this holy democracy of all creatures is the privilege and task of partnership with the Holy One in the work of creation. To understand biodiversity as an expression of the worldview of Torah, one must look to biblical/rabbinic tradition and to its grand, sweeping stories of what creation means. Let us look once more to the Beginning, at the opening of the book of Genesis, and to the great modification and re-creation that was the Flood.

Several additional features of the creation story inform a Jewish understanding of biodiversity. The first is the emphatic repetition of *le-mineihu* (its own kind): "God said: Let the earth sprout forth with sprouting-growth, plants that seed forth seeds, fruit trees that yield fruit, after their kind [*le-mino*].... God saw that it was good" (Genesis 1:11–12). Notice that at each stage of creation, the creatures participate in creation, are co-creators. Each brings forth its own descendants, in response to the divine lure, expressing both the divine invitation and each species' unique *chokhmah*, characteristic wisdom. Again, "God created the great sea-serpents and all living things that crawl about, with which the waters swarmed, after their kind [*le-mineihem*], and all winged fowl after their kind [*le-mineihu*]. God saw that it was good" (Genesis 1:21). "God made the wildlife of the earth after their kind [*le-minah*], and the herd-animals after their kind [*le-minah*], and all crawling things of the soil after their kind [*le-mineihu*]. God saw it was good" (Genesis 1:25).

The repetition of "its own kind" and the immediate judgment that these categories are good affirms the importance of the diversity of living things. Each type of plant and animal contributes to the cumulative goodness of God's creation. The establishment of each new type brings divine delight, a further embodiment of the divine zest for life. Each new species adds something beneficial and necessary to the world. As the psalmist notes, "How great Your works, Holy One; in wisdom have You made them all" (Psalm 104:24).

The Sages note that the Torah's creation story teaches us to recognize that humanity does not have pride of place in creation; God does. Humans were not created first "so they should not grow proud—for one can say to them, 'The gnat came before you in the creation'!" (Talmud, *Sanhedrin* 38a).[9] The Sages compare the way God prepared the world for us to "a ruler who built a palace, dedicated it, prepared a meal, and only then invited the guests" (Talmud, *Sanhedrin* 38a). Humanity is a guest in God's world: "The earth and its fullness belong to the Holy One" (Psalm 24:1). Creation, with all its diversity, reflects great wisdom and foresight. Those species are not ours to abuse or destroy, since they—and we—belong to the Holy One. A contemporary reading of the creation stories should enhance our sense of reverence for all creation, our humility in the face of God's wondrous ongoing work, a resolve to serve on behalf of the ongoing vitality of creation as a whole, and celebration of the diversity God and we so cherish.

Humanity as Guardian of Diversity

Those same values—of humility and awe—emerge from the story of the Flood and Noah's ark. "The earth had gone to ruin before God, the earth was filled with wrongdoing. God saw the earth, and here: it had gone to ruin, for all flesh had ruined its way upon the earth" (Genesis 6:11–12). Here the Torah deliberately updates itself: God's act of creation is very good, but the chaotic abuse by humanity has ruined it! Our actions have not only ruined the earth for ourselves, but they have also imposed unwanted consequences on all living creatures: "All the residents of the world are governed by one and the same destiny."[10] In an attempt to restore creation, God resolves to send a flood and instructs Noah, "a righteous, wholehearted man" (Genesis 6:9), to construct an ark:

> From all (ritually) pure animals you are to take seven and seven (each), a male and his mate, and from all the animals that are not pure, two (each), a male and his mate, and also from the fowl of the heavens, seven and seven (each), male and female, to keep seed alive upon the face of all the earth. (Genesis 7:2–3)

Such a command can only make sense if the survival of living diversity matters. Indeed, rabbinic tradition articulates that value through a midrash in which the dove chastises Noah for endangering the survival of doves as a species:

> "You must hate me, for you did not choose from the species of which there are seven [in the ark], but from the species of which there are only two. If the power of the sun or the power of cold overwhelmed me, would not the world be lacking a species?" (Talmud, *Sanhedrin* 108b)[11]

The story of Noah's ark powerfully affirms the value of each existent species and highlights the role of humanity as God's partner in the preservation of biodiversity, despite our ability to threaten that same variety.

Diversity Enshrined in Jewish Law

The value of biodiversity that undergirds two of the stories of the Hebrew Bible also finds repeated expression in the application of *halakhah* (Jewish law). Just as the *mitzvot* generally concretize the values of *aggadah* (narrative), here too Jewish law expresses the importance of diversity through the pedagogy of mandated action. The *mitzvot* symbolize, embody, and implement our most sacred commitments as Jews. Rabbinic tradition understands the *mitzvot* that follow as reminders of the value of maintaining species diversity and as an agenda for actually preserving them:

- *Kilayim*: This category of Jewish law prohibits mixing diverse species together. It covers six kinds of mixed species: mixed seeds, grafting trees, seeds in a vineyard, crossbreeding animals, pulling cattle, and mixing linen and wool in garments (*sha'atnez*).[12] *Kilayim* is prohibited by *halakhah* as an unwarranted tampering with the categories established by God's creation. In a similar vein, the Jerusalem Talmud understands the biblical verse "My statutes you shall keep" (Leviticus 19:19) as referring to "the statutes I have engraved in the world" (Jerusalem Talmud, *Kilayim* 1:7)—in other words, a reverence for the ways of natural entities. Ramban, the great medieval philosopher and sage, explains, "God has created in the world various species among all living things, both plants and moving creatures, and God gave them the power of reproduction, enabling them to exist forever as long as the Blessed God will desire the existence of the world."[13] The prohibition of *kilayim* is an affirmation of species and diversity in the world as we find it.

- Sending the Mother Bird Away: The Torah records the insistence that one who gathers eggs from a nest must first shoo the mother away (Deuteronomy 22:6–7). While the Torah does not reveal a reason for this practice, medieval rabbis were emphatic in linking this *mitzvah* to the preservation of species. In the *Sefer Ha-Chinnukh*, we are told that "God's desire is for the endurance of God's species ... for under the watchful care of the One who lives and endures forever ... it [every species] will find enduring existence through God."[14] Ramban speculates that "it may be that scripture does not permit us to destroy a species altogether, although it permits slaughter [for food] within that group. Now, one who kills the dam and the young in one day, or takes them when they are free to fly, it is as though he cut off that species."[15] Both of these authoritative rabbis understand this *mitzvah* as demonstrating the importance of maintaining each species of plant and animal. Jewish conduct must support the divine intention that each species thrive.

- Slaughtering the Animal and Its Young: Leviticus 22:28 prohibits slaughtering the mother ox or sheep and her young on the same day. As with the rule about releasing the mother bird, this law was understood in terms of ensuring the continuation of existent species. In this area, Jewish thinkers articulate an explicit notion that providence pertains to entire species. Just as environmental ethics values the species over the individual member of the species, Jewish thought insists that each species of animal has a "right" to exist that comes from, and is protected by, God. In the words of *Sefer Ha-Chinnukh*, "One should reflect that the watchful care of the Blessed God extends to all the species of living creatures generally, and with God's providential concern for them they will endure permanently."[16]

- Kashrut, the Dietary Laws: While the dietary laws do not speak directly to the issue of biodiversity, they do express the biblical emphasis on species as categories deserving attention and respect. In two separate lists (Leviticus 11 and Deuteronomy 14), the Torah delineates categories of animals that may and may not be eaten. One thoughtful scholar has suggested that the categories of *tahor* (pure) and *tamei* (impure) actually tell us what part of creation is available for our use (what we call "pure") and what part is not authorized for human benefit (what we call "impure").[17] That remarkable observation highlights that Judaism sees much of creation as existing for the satisfaction and self-expression of God and creation, not just for humanity. Jews are not allowed to eat most animal species, and designating them as *tamei* reminds the traditionally observant Jew that the purpose of the world is not exclusively to please people. As the Midrash notes, "It is not thanks to you that rain falls, or that the sun shines—it is thanks to the animals" (*Genesis Rabbah* 33:1).

Each of these *mitzvot* directs Jews to demonstrate their reverence for creation as it is. Taken together, they form an embodied essay in deeds on the subject of serving the Creator by maintaining the creation as we find it. If God made all these species deliberately, we can do no less than assist in their continuing vitality. If God's loving care extends over the range of living things, our love must be sufficiently strong to keep them alive—as a tribute to our Creator, as the best defense for our own survival, and as an abiding expression of our love of life.

Life Is a Symphony

In our role as partners, humanity can preserve the diversity of living creatures. Embodied in forms ever more intricate and diverse, life becomes a polyphonic symphony in praise of its Source.

> *Praise God, sun and moon,*
> *Praise God, all bright stars...!*
> *Praise Adonai, all who are on the earth,*
> *All sea monsters and ocean depths ...*
> *All mountains and hills,*
> *All fruit trees and cedars,*
> *All wild and tamed beasts,*
> *Creeping things and winged birds,*
> *All monarchs and peoples of the earth!*
> (*Psalm 148:3–11*)

The more the types of instruments, the more intriguing the melody; the more the number of species, the more resplendent the creation.

The kabbalists saw biodiversity not in terms of a symphony at work but of a congregation at prayer. In the words of Rabbi Nachman of Breslov, "Every blade of grass sings poetry to God,"[18] and Rabbi

Abraham Isaac Kook affirmed that "everything that grows says something, every stone whispers some secret, all creation sings."[19] For creation to function as a congregation, humanity must train ourselves to identify with all creatures and with all creation. We must discipline our desires and work for the well-being of the whole.

God's unity pervades creation: all are connected to each, and each to all. The unity of what God has created envelops us, providing us with context and with goal. The diversity of all living things constitutes yet another rainbow, in which each species' distinctiveness adds to the resplendence of the totality, and in which any group's extinction impoverishes and endangers the rest.

At present, the oneness of all living things is hidden, masked by our species' self-reliance and self-regard. But the illusion of humanity's dominion, maintained by our selfishness and delusions of power, will one day give way before the unification of God and God's name. That vision of unity, of a time in which God, humanity, and the rest of creation live together in reverent balance, is as contemporary as environmental ethics and as ancient as scripture. Our covenant, as Jews and as God's partners in the work of creation, impels us to ensure the flourishing of the diversity of all creatures. Our calling, as Jews and as caretakers, is to exert our best efforts to protect all of life and to fortify our faith in the bounteous flowering of life and, when the time comes, in the faithful embrace of death.

Creation and Death

Joining the Cycle of Life

Indeed, people are but grass:
Grass withers, flowers fade—
But the word of our God is always fulfilled!"
—Isaiah 40:6–8

The bounteous flowering of life is part of a larger cycle, the intricate dance of natality and mortality, of birth and of death.[1] An embodied, emergent understanding of the process of creation directs our attention not merely to birth and vitality, but also to life's endings.

When I was a congregational rabbi in Orange County, California, I loved looking through the window of my synagogue study, enjoying a vista of a dense, tree-covered, sloping hill and valley that my suburban community preserved as green space. Still sporting the wild plants that originally graced it, that valley and hill grounded me in the larger purpose of my work—consciously living with the reality of creation, cultivating gratitude in the Creator of all this teeming life, and guiding others to understand their spiritual responsibility and opportunity to be co-creators, both as people and as Jews. I took great comfort in that view, because it elicited, through good times and bad, the majesty, richness, and continuity of life. The occasional sighting of a mother coyote with her twin pups reminded me that we are less distant from other living things than we might like to assume and that simply being in the world connects us to something vast and beautiful.

From that same window, past the hills to the nearby road, I occasionally spotted the mutilated bodies of possums, cats, and birds struck by the cars that raced by with such reckless haste. Adjacent to the lush, thriving vegetation, the concrete arteries of our transportation—a resource that makes much of our living possible—regularly claims the lives of the denizens of the woods. Life and death, woods and pavement jostle side by side, linked in a dance in which each player takes its turn, in which no one partner can hope to dominate forever. Life, then death, then life, then death follow each other in a cycle, sketching a pattern greater than any individual can ever hope to transcend.

As a rabbi, I was used to watching that cycle flow by. Funerals, unveilings, bar and bat mitzvahs, baby namings, hospital visits, and ritual circumcisions form the weft and warp of my calendar. During Torah readings, the very basis of Jewish communal living, we pray for the sick, recall the dead, bless newlyweds, and name new generations of babies. These prayers, recollections, and celebrations constitute no interruption of the reading; rather, they incorporate the words of Torah into the living reality of actual lives as lived, and as mourned. As with the view from my study, so too the view from the sanctuary: life and death, biology and culture, nature and artifice are intertwined in religion as they are in life.

My rabbinic life throws me into the thick of life's tangles, making all moments of the life cycle contemporaneous and inseparable. An awareness of life's vastness and relentlessness is nothing new: I have driven from a funeral to a *brit milah* and finished the day with a wedding party followed by a shiva minyan. Life, before my eyes, parades whole and haphazardly. I imagine it must look that way to God, too: "In Your sight a thousand years are like yesterday that has passed like a watch in the night" (Psalm 90:4). Thanks to my life embedded in a diverse community, I have noticed life's panorama, begun to consider its implications, to read the world, as it were. Immersing myself in the literature of environmental ethics and Process Thought, I have begun to see the trees for the forest, for all forests. The combination of these systemic ways of thinking about the world coupled with the welter of life's raucous encounters have opened me to feeling my place in creation as a religious act, as a source for knowing God in a deeper, more nuanced way:

> *I see You in the starry field,*
>
> *I see You in the harvest's yield,*
>
> *In every breath, in every sound,*
>
> *An echo of Your name is found.*
>
> *The blade of grass, the simple flower,*
>
> *Bear witness to Your matchless power,*
>
> *In wonder-working, or some bush aflame,*
>
> *We look for God and fancy You concealed:*
>
> *But in earth's common things You stand revealed*
>
> *While grass and flowers and stars spell out Your name.*[2]

That new way has led to an unanticipated connection between the ways our culture denies death—and hence cowers in paralyzing fear of it—and the way we also blind ourselves to creation—and hence are terrified and contemptuous of the realities of life on the planet Earth. I believe that our obsession with denying both death and planetary considerations, the pretense that we live forever and that we can use the world's riches in any way we please, emerges from the same underlying insecurity and responds to a particularly human shallowness that threatens both the quality of life and our ability to function unimpaired in the world.

Permit me a rabbinic illustration: Many adults report to me that they have never been to a funeral, even well into midlife. As a society, we have so successfully quarantined death from life that one can reach midlife without being present at the moment of someone's death, without personally seeing a corpse or a casket, without having assumed an obligation for personally comforting a mourner. Most people do not want to think about the inevitability of death, which means that most refuse to make any preparations in advance (which, in turn, entails that the bereaved are forced to focus on some gruesome business decisions during the time of their sharpest grief).

While Jews—along with other Americans—routinely distance themselves from death and dying, Judaism, as a way of life, has always insisted on an intimacy between the living and the dead that would shock many moderns. Jewish law insists that the dying are not to be left alone, that no one should have to die without their loved ones and community on hand every step of the way.[3] The corpse is to be bathed and clothed by members of that community— generally volunteers[4]—and burial is traditionally quick[5] and simple: dressed in a shroud,[6] the remains of the dead are buried directly into the ground, without coffin,[7] without flowers, without anything interfering in the return of the body to the earth. Mourners are to escort the remains to the graveside,[8] and the immediate family and friends consider it an act of love, a privilege, to bury their loved one themselves.[9] A Jew, having died, is to be embraced by the earth and the community at the same time, in yet another harmonious partnership between creation and covenant. The God of Torah is also the Source of life and death.

That integration is no longer the norm. In fact, in many places it is not even a possibility. The primary factor for many cemeteries is the appearance of the lawn, itself an unnatural import in many locales. In order to preserve the surreal quality of cemetery lawns, not only are bodies placed inside coffins, but also those coffins are then lowered into almost airtight cement boxes. When I first started working as a congregational rabbi, the cemeteries often used what they called a bell liner, a concrete cover shaped like a bell that simply fit over the casket. While its primary purpose was to prevent the collapse of the grave with the passage of time, at least the bell liner allowed direct contact between the earth and the casket. Increasingly, however, cemeteries use a two-thousand-pound, two-piece concrete box that resembles nothing other than a giant shoebox. The bottom piece rests in the grave before the coffin is lowered into it, and the top—conveyed by crane—settles heavily above the casket after the mourners have already left. That way they do not have to witness the final indignity: their loved one's remains are hermetically sealed inside walls of concrete for millennia—the final deception.

At one funeral I performed, just after a cleansing rain that left the skies crystal blue and the ground sated and damp, I asked the funeral director why they used this new concrete box instead of the bell liner. I was told, "Most families do not want to see the casket lowered into water." Fear of death and separation from creation coalesced in a burial that precluded the reunification of earthly remains with the earth, shattering the comfort that might have come from knowing that this death would lead to new life, that this body would provide the basis for new life and new beginnings.

Our fear of death and our desire to disguise it has created something truly terrifying. Our blindness to creation and its rhythms has produced a practice unnatural and unnerving. Even in death, a wall of concrete now blocks our loved ones from a more wholesome unity with the earth and with life's regeneration and resurrection.

Both our panic and our audacity spring from the same source, just as insecurity is often the lurking motivation of the bully. We humans, terrified to recognize our own dependency, our own creatureliness, bully the world with our swaggering denial of death, with our supposed freedom to dominate the world and all it contains. But our bravado rings false. Just as the brutality of the bully only reimposes a terrible loneliness and a self-fulfilling sense of being misunderstood, our futile manipulation of nature and our desperate attempts to deny death can only deepen our misery, our isolation, and the very dependency we sought to avoid in the first place.

Are we trapped, then, within an ever-accelerating cycle of fleeing our fears and pretensions and being further enmeshed by them? Is there no alternative to our alienation from our natures and all nature?

Denying reality will never provide us comfort. Instead, the intrusion of the inevitable keeps us in need of an ever more powerful and desperate illusion, one that must fail in its turn as well. As our illusions languish in succession, the realities underlying our fears only grow more gripping and implacable.

Rather than denying reality, an effort doomed from the start, a more fruitful approach would suggest opening ourselves to the possibility of beginning with reality and grounding ourselves, literally and ideologically, within the fertile soil of creation. Instead of shielding ourselves from death, we can understand the end of our current embodied existence as an intrinsic part of life, one with value for our progeny, our planet, and ourselves. Rather than shutting ourselves behind walls of concrete, or living our lives behind walls of any kind, we can open ourselves to the world in which we live, the one from which we borrow and to which we must inevitably return.

Life, larger and more encompassing than any particular expression of living, than any one embodiment of its vitality, is a process that connects us to each other, to past and future, and to all created things. It is primal; eluding both thought and word, the process of life and death transcends language and culture. Its sheer energy, force, and drive are both terrifying and liberating. We take up the very elements that had been used to sustain earlier living occasions and some day relinquish our hold on those resources so that new life may flourish in its time. Perhaps that is why one of the traditional phrases for death is *shavak chayim lekhol chai*, "to surrender life for all the living."[10] Our willingness to propagate and our love for the generations yet to come impel a willingness to mortality, to providing the resources to sustain the young lives we love, in whom we see our hopes, our dreams, and our salvation.

One generation makes room for the next. When God tells Moses that he must die, Moses (even Moses!) pleads for immortality. According to the Midrash, God responds, "Moses, I have bound Myself with an oath that no [mortal] reign shall overlap another by even a hair's breadth. Up until now you were king over Israel; now it is the time for Joshua to be king over them."[11] The emergence of new life requires the recycling of the old; the new generation cannot have its moments without the passing of the previous age. If we love our children, we have to let go: "There is a time for being born and a time for dying" (Ecclesiastes 3:2).

We cannot control the world, try as we often do. As the Rabbis of the Mishnah recognize, "It was not your will that formed you, nor was it your will that gave you birth. It is not your will that makes you live, and it is not your will that brings you death" (*Mishnah Avot* 4:29).[12] We cannot make cosmic decisions of life and death, of necessity and value, when so much of the complexity of life and its interrelationships eludes our understanding and snares us in the very web we seek to weave. In asserting a false control, like a fly seeking to escape a spider, our ever more desperate remedies fling us closer and closer to our end. In our growing danger, our rising panic prevents the patience, the calm so necessary for vision, perspective, and comfort.

Where can we look, then, for our help? To whom can we turn for that broader vision and timeless perspective?

If we start by acknowledging our embeddedness in creation and our dependence on the rest of creation and the Creator, we may hope to abandon our futile attempts to master the world through coercive manipulation or brute force. Einstein taught us that the position of the viewer alters what is viewed. We are, ourselves, within creation, expressive of creation, in process. This insight cautions us against the deception of mastering creation, since our efforts must simultaneously shift the complex equations and surroundings that control our own lives.

Because we cannot step outside of life to view it from a neutral place, because there is no external base on which to place the fulcrum to lift the world, our first reality—and our last—is one of belonging, of symbiosis. We *are* the world, at least in part. We reflect the divine image of God, but we do so as creatures, not as gods. Whatever comfort may be ours must issue from that recognition, from that humble sense of place.

Admitting God as our Creator and the Creator of all allows us—as partners with God in maintaining the work of creation and as creatures fashioned through eons of emergent evolution to live in the world—to be ourselves: to seek more realistic and modest goals with which to establish meaning in our lives and significance for our deeds.

We can rise to our potential if we recognize that our mandate is but to maintain and to shepherd creation. Just as the Torah and Jewish law authorize doctors only to heal and to comfort,[13] so humanity, as the physicians of creation, work authentically and faithfully when we sustain the functioning of a system too complex to master and too beautiful to control. Our success is to be measured by how well we can care for the least among us and for the world in which we live. We succeed when we maintain community or establish a new fellowship, a communion with those whom we previously rejected as "other" or as "outside." We establish communion not only with all living things before us but also with our progeny—and all living things who will succeed us. In the words of the philosopher Hans Jonas:

> So let us be Jews also in this. With young life pressing after us, we can grow old and sated with days, resign ourselves to death—giving youth and therewith life a new chance. In acknowledging his finitude under God, a Jew, if he is still a Jew, must be able to say with the Psalmist:
>
>> We bring our years to an end as a tale that is told
>> The days of our years are threescore years and ten,
>> Or even by reason of strength fourscore years....
>> So teach us to number our days,
>> That we may get us a heart of wisdom.
>>   (Psalm 90:10–12)[14]

Death loses some of its sting if our more modest sense of self displaces the arrogant delusion of being essential: I do, indeed, need the world and living creatures, but they do not need me—at least not forever. I need creation as the garden in which to exult, grow, play, work, struggle, learn, and sing. As a part of creation, there is a sense in which creation needs me, but only to the degree that I am a willing participant of that creation, an expression of its vitality, and a partner in its process. Once I separate myself from the world, once I sever my embeddedness in creation, then I set myself up against it and creation no longer needs me. I make myself an alien, requiring the reinforcement of concrete and the glitter of acquisitions to hold my delusions in place.

An embodied, emergent vision of the world as process—as God and creation's continuous handiwork—and of humanity—as God's caretakers and the physicians of all creation—allows us to transcend our crippling fear of death and our deadly alienation from the rest of creation. We are a part of the world, not apart from it, and our lives join the shimmering waves of an endless sea. We flow from it, and return to it, and in that cycle of tide and tow, of ebb and flow, we leave a mark precisely to the degree that the sea continues, unimpeded, on its way. We die to new life, for new life. And in death we are embraced by the earth and by God, if we but have the courage to open our arms.

Part V

LOCATING OURSELVES
Israel and the World

The land shall be holy....
—Leviticus 27:21

Embraced by the earth in death, we embrace the earth throughout our lifetimes, both as emergent children of the whole earth and carrying at the same time our yearning for and belonging to a particular place—*Eretz Yisrael*, the Land of Israel. How we integrate these two ways of loving the land grounds our embodied existence, as Jews, as people, as partners with God in the work of creation.[1] That integration—love of the earth and a particular love of one special place, Israel—forms the subject matter of this section. Any Jewish consideration of creation must focus on land not in the abstract, but as the tangible soil of our very embodiment. Not just earth as an ideal, but as a particular planet, *the* Earth; not land as abstraction, but a particular land, the Land of Israel. This perspective concretizes our belonging to the earth and our carrying its consciousness into human discourse and action.

Jewish tradition speaks at great length about the sanctity of the earth and its produce.[2] However, while the biblical notion of holiness emphasizes the Land of Israel, rabbinic writings expand that notion to include all lands, the planet Earth. While the Rabbis do not deny the particular holiness of *Eretz Yisrael*, their writings make the sanctification of all the earth incumbent upon Jews as a matter of religious duty. So in this final section, we bring it all together: love of the earth as a whole and passion for a particular place, the Land of Israel, as our portal to a grounded life.

15

Territory Without Map
The Sanctity of Soil

> One generation passes away, and another generation
> comes, but the earth abides forever.
> —Ecclesiastes 1:4

Jewish tradition is especially rich in its attention to the sanctity of the Land (*kedushat ha-aretz*), of Israel.[1] Attention to the earth as a place of religious meaning pervades the Hebrew Bible.[2] The creation narratives focus attention on the importance of the earth, to the extent that the term itself, *adamah*, lends its name to the ultimate earthling, Adam.[3] The theme of creation, emphasizing God's sovereignty over the entire planet, repeats itself in several prophetic passages as well. Isaiah urges his audience:

> *Lift high your eyes and see:*
>
> *Who created these?*
>
> *One who sends out their host by count,*
>
> *Who calls them each by name:*
>
> *Because of God's great might and vast power,*
>
> *Not one fails to appear. (Isaiah 40:26)[4]*

Moses, standing before the burning bush on Horeb (another biblical name for Mount Sinai), receives the command to "remove your sandals from your feet, for the place on which you stand is holy ground"

(Exodus 3:5). The same ideology that portrays God as Creator of the heavens and the earth also establishes a link between all lands and God. Perhaps this appreciation of the entire planet as the creation of the loving God also contributes to the venerable Israelite tradition extolling the wilderness as a place of holiness and purity.[5] As the source of all places, God's sanctity must somehow touch every place.

The Land of Israel and the Hebrew Bible

Yet there is a dipolarity at the core of the biblical understandings of the sanctity of soil. The whole world may be sacred, but one particular part of it boasts a special degree of holiness. While Israelites can observe their laws anywhere (Psalm 105:44–45), there is an uncleanness that permeates the lands of the world.[6] Thus Hosea speaks of the Israelites who "shall eat unclean food in Assyria" (Hosea 9:3),[7] and Amos portrays the "unclean soil" to which Israel will be banished (Amos 7:17).[8] The Land of Israel is clearly the focus of the Hebrew Bible's passion for land.

Repeatedly, the Torah describes the Land of Israel as "a good land" (e.g., Deuteronomy 8:7–10), one whose bounty reflects God's beneficence, not the result of any merit or labor on Israel's part (Joshua 24:13). The sanctity of *Eretz Yisrael* overrides the sanctity of all other places; it is only in ancient, preconquest times "that a site outside the Promised Land can be described as holy."[9] So sacred is the Land that Jews may offer sacrifices only there, and only there is food considered ritually clean for sacrifices, although not for eating. Throughout the *Tanakh*, the Land represents both promise *and* goal; Israel observes the *mitzvot* in order to merit the Land.

Paradoxically, God's sovereignty over the Land of Israel emerges from the creation story itself. God made everything. Therefore, all lands, Israel included, belong to God.[10] In the book of Leviticus, that reasoning provides the base for God's inalienable ownership of the Land:

> The Land must not be sold beyond reclaim, for the Land is Mine; you are but strangers resident with Me. Throughout the

land that you hold you must provide for the redemption of
the Land. (Leviticus 25:23–24)[11]

God's ownership of the earth is total, and the selection of Israel is a
divine prerogative.

The distinction of the Land of Israel is but one consequence of
God's role as creator. Obeying or violating God's will entails immediate consequences for continued existence and well-being on the
Land. A series of agricultural laws—*pe'ah* (law requiring the corners
of the crop to be left standing for the poor),[12] *orlah* (law prohibiting
produce of a tree for the first three years),[13] *terumot* (law specifying
donation of a percentage of one's crops to the Levites and to the
poor),[14] and *bikkurim* (law requiring the first produce of a harvest
offered as a sacred gift)[15]—provide repeated evidence of God's ownership of the Land of Israel.

That the human farmer is but a tenant undergirds all of these
requirements—of abstention, of Temple donation, or of provision
for the poor. The ultimate proprietor is God alone. In the words of
the Talmud, "God acquired possession of the world and apportioned
it to humanity, but God always remains the master of the world"
(Talmud, *Rosh Ha-Shanah* 31a).

The consequences of violating God's will also link *Eretz Yisrael*
to the rest of the earth. Many passages warn that expulsion from the
Land is the price of scorning the *mitzvot*.[16] In good Process perspective, the Land is not seen as inert or mechanical; rather, the earth's
soil is living and responsive, and there is a dynamic between the people Israel and their Land. Acts of hostility toward God result in acts
of hostility toward the actors themselves. The earth is not only a witness to the covenant[17] but also a participant in the unfolding drama
of righteousness, chastisement, and rebuke. Other nations, as well as
the Land of Israel, share that involvement:

> *The earth is withered, sear;*
> *The world languishes, it is sear;*

The most exalted people of the earth languish.

For the earth was defiled

Under its inhabitants;

Because they transgressed teachings,

Violated laws,

Broke the ancient covenant. (Isaiah 24:4–5)

The biblical view of the world is not distant or objective; it demands immediate involvement and consequence.[18]

> [That] observance and non-observance of the command-
> ments have geographic, territorial, and cosmic consequences
> points to the truth that ecology is indissoluble from morality,
> land and law being mutually dependent, and that a people is
> ultimately responsible for the maintenance of its "place."[19]

In short, the biblical conceptions of the relationship between the people Israel and the Land of Israel express covenant.

The Land of Israel and Rabbinic Wisdom

Rabbinic law and legend also stress the centrality of *Eretz Yisrael*. In the words of *Mishnah Keilim* 1:6, "The Land of Israel is holier than all [other] lands." Far more than in scripture, large sections of the Mishnah are devoted to the agricultural laws of tithing,[20] which are obligatory only within the Land (with the exception of *kilayim* [the prohibition of crossbreeding seeds and animals and mixing wool and linen], *orlah*, and, according to Rabbi Eliezer, eating barley before the *omer*).[21] Further, the purity system is fully applicable only within the Land.[22] Consequently, the impurity of the other lands—a notion that has roots in the Hebrew Bible—continues into rabbinic thought as well.[23]

Portable Holiness

Often the Mishnah postulates the overlap of the people Israel and the Land, the two primary concentrations of holiness. Even within the Tannaitic period, however, the existence of significant Jewish populations in Syria, Egypt, and Babylonia required some adjustments to the notion of a single holy Land. Although the people Israel in the Land of Israel (*Am Yisrael be-Eretz Yisrael*) remains the ideal, a growing number of cases require distinctions previously unnecessary in biblical thought. For example, gentiles living in the Land are exempt from the requirements of *shevi'it* (the law of the Sabbatical year), *challah* (the law of a dough offering), and *terumah* (food offering for the priests).[24] This adjustment reflects a new reality, that the "Mishnah's Rabbis clearly wish to do justice to both principles, Holy Land *and* Holy People, without fully embracing the one over the other."[25]

A similar readjustment is reflected in a dispute between two early rabbis over whether produce exported from the Land of Israel requires taking *challah*. Rabbi Eliezer insists that it does, implying a single source of holiness emanating from Zion. Rabbi Akiva, however, postulates a conception of multiple holiness by ruling that such produce is exempt. For Rabbi Akiva:

> The entire world potentially is sacred space. Different areas are subject to different standards, different rules. People in the Land and outside the Land alike have their own special roles to play. Quite clearly later Rabbinic traditions follow Akiva's lead, enlarging the scope of the investigation of what the individual's roles should be, in different places, but especially outside the Land, and at different times. The goal is perception of everyday life as participation in a sacred realm of ultimate significance.[26]

Reiterating the sanctity of other lands exercises a profound effect on Rabbinic Judaism, reinforcing the portable holiness that Jews take with them wherever they dwell. That recognition of the sanctity of land beyond *Eretz Yisrael* provides for halakhic accommodation of Jewish communities in Syria (*Mishnah Challah* 4:11) as well as one prominent opinion prohibiting *aliyah* from Babylonia to Israel:

> Whoever goes up from Babylonia to the Land of Israel trans-
> gresses an imperative commandment, for it is said in scrip-
> tures, "They shall be carried to Babylonia, and there shall
> they be, until the day that I remember them, says the Holy
> One (Jeremiah 27:22)." (Talmud, *Ketubot* 110b–111a)

Rabbi Judah even goes so far as to equate living in Babylonia with
living in Israel (Talmud, *Ketubot* 110b).

These views reflect a specific rabbinic agenda: to align Jewish
religion to the reality of Jewish settlement beyond the borders of the
Land of Israel. Without ever abandoning their commitment to the
mitzvah of settling the Land (*yishuv ha-aretz*), the Sages transferred
their ideal from living on the Land to observing the teaching.[27]
Whereas the Torah esteems living in Israel as the goal of pious observance, the Rabbis invert that estimation; they cherish living on the
Land *because* it allows for greater observance. Here the Land does not
embody the goal; the Land becomes the means:

> Rabbi Simlai expounded, "Why did Moses our Rabbi yearn
> to enter the Land of Israel? Did he want to eat of its fruit or
> satisfy himself from its bounty? But thus spoke Moses, 'Many
> commandments were commanded to Israel that can be ful-
> filled only in the Land of Israel. I wish to enter the Land so
> they may all be fulfilled by me.'" (Talmud, *Sotah* 14a).[28]

The re-estimation of the virtue of settling the Land (*yishuv ha-aretz*)
maintains the centrality of the Land of Israel, since certain *mitzvot*
can be fulfilled only there, but shifts the weight of Jewish piety to
the observance of deeds that can be performed anywhere.[29] The liturgy of the seasons reflects this alteration, emphasizing the needs
of Babylonia and concentrating the attention of other Jewish communities on their rhythm as a distinctly religious concern.[30] The
calendar—long a source of contention between the Sages of Israel
and those of Babylonia—presents a similar struggle, with authority
ultimately taken by the Ge'onim (the supreme religious authorities)

of Babylonia.[31] Perhaps as early as the canonization of the Torah in the Second Temple period, but certainly following the destruction of the Temple and the rise of the synagogue, Rabbinic Judaism adopted an attitude of provisional portability: a willingness to roam the world until the messianic age restores the nexus between Land and people:

> What the Mishnah does by presenting this cult, laying out its measurements, describing its rite, and specifying its rules, is to permit Israel, in the words of the Mishnah, to experience anywhere and anytime that cosmic center of the world described by the Mishnah: cosmic center in words made utopia.[32]

The Earth
Is the Holy One's
Blessings for Food

You shall eat there before the Holy One your God,
and you shall rejoice in all that you put your hand to.
—Deuteronomy 12:7

The Rabbis of the Mishnah and the Talmud established two overlapping systems of dual holiness (the Land of Israel and the people Israel, the Land of Israel and the entire earth). This dual geography of holiness becomes clear with the example of the blessings recited before eating different types of food (*birkhot ha-nehenin*).[1]

Understanding the significance of specific blessings (singular, *berakhah*; plural, *berakhot*) requires a moment's reflection on the social importance of structure and of categorization. Meaning is not intrinsic; the people involved confer it. This is just one more example of the profound Process insight that meaning emerges only in the context of relationships, among people, or between people and a place. A ritual, for example, reveals little about the role that ritual plays in the life of those engaged in it unless the words and intentions of the participants of the rite are also available. While investigating meaning, "the thing to ask is not what their ontological status is ... the thing to ask is what their import is: what it is ... that in their occurrence and through their agency, is getting said."[2]

One key to unlocking the significance of a ritual, as with other social rites, is what it can reveal about a context of understanding how the worshipers construe the world around them and their place in it.

Ritual not only reveals structures of perception and purpose. It also helps shape that purpose: "Ritual did not merely encode ideas that could be expressed otherwise; rather, it created the essential categories of human thought."[3] When a recitation or symbolic action expresses a value concept, that performance not only articulates a specific way of seeing the world; it also shapes and reinforces that vision. In our case, an examination of rabbinic blessings for food reveals the effort to recognize the sanctity of the entire planet, to ground that holiness in God's ownership, and to maintain the special status of the Land of Israel.

The biblical command to praise God for food specifies that this obligation applies only within the Land of Israel: "For the Holy One your God is bringing you into a good land ... a land where you may eat food without stint.... When you have eaten your fill, give thanks to the Holy One your God for the good land which God has given you" (Deuteronomy 8:7, 8:9–10). There is no explicit biblical implementation, but the clear assumption behind this instruction is that the Land of Israel is uniquely holy and that the landedness of the Jews rightly elicits a distinctive gratitude. Food grown in God's land requires a means to transfer ownership from God to humanity. Blessings, in this understanding, represent a delivery system by which food in its naturally sanctified state of nature is removed from that natural habitat not only physically but also conceptually, so that it may be transformed for use by ordinary human beings.[4]

To eat without blessing, according to the Rabbis, is not only theft. It also represents a desecration of the Temple-based system of purity and holiness:

> Our Rabbis taught: It is forbidden to enjoy anything of this
> world without a *berakhah*, and whoever enjoys anything of
> this world without a *berakhah* commits sacrilege [*ma'al*].
> Rav Judah said in the name of Samuel: To enjoy anything of
> this world without a *berakhah* is like making personal use of
> things consecrated to heaven. (Talmud, *Berakhot* 35a)[5]

The Rabbis' assumption that blessings are appropriate both in and out of the Land should be noted from the outset. They place no limitation on the location of the meal or the source of the produce to be consumed. The Torah prescribes gratitude to God as Sovereign of Israel; the Rabbis extend that response to the world:

> It is written: "The earth is the Holy One's and the fullness
> thereof" (Psalm 24:1), yet "God has given the earth to human
> beings" (Psalm 115:16). There is no contradiction. The first
> verse reflects the situation before we say a blessing, whereas
> the second verse applies after the blessing has been recited.
> (Talmud, *Berakhot* 35a)

Characteristic of their ability to mediate a complex agenda, the Rabbis also reinforce the notion of the Land's sanctity (*kedushat ha-aretz*) through the insertion of specific *berakhot* in the Blessing after Meals (*Birkat Ha-Mazon*) and the Shorter Blessing after Meals (*Berakhah Achat Mei-ein Shalosh*), both of which distinguish between produce characteristic of the Land and all other produce. Yet the actual source of the grains, fruit, or vegetables is now irrelevant. What counts is that their species grows in *Eretz Yisrael*.

Blessings Grow from the Ground

In at least one other significant way, the series of blessings over food sanctifies the entire earth. The central organizing category that distinguishes which type of *berakhah* to recite is whether (and, if so, how) food emerges from the soil. Once the produce is identified as a type of fruit, further distinctions arise: Does the food emerge from the earth directly, or does it grow on a vine or tree? Other possible categorizations seem not to matter. "Over something that does not grow from the earth, one says, *she-ha-kol*" (*Mishnah Berakhot* 6:3).

There is no necessary or intrinsic reason to worry about the nuances of distinct agricultural products while lumping together fish, meat, and poultry. By establishing the categories of *berakhot* the way they did, the Rabbis lent significance to the soil, to what emerges from the ground, and to the sanctity of all ground everywhere. The categories of the *berakhot* themselves valorize the earth as a sacred and sustaining presence. "Blessings achieve the primal function of freeing that produce from its sacred state."[6] They also enforce the insight that a sacred place is anywhere that life can thrive, that a sacred time is anytime Jews gather to eat and to pray.

Responsibility for Our "Place"
The Earth Is in Our Hands

> I found the world provided with carob trees since
> my ancestors planted them for me. Now I am
> planting them for my descendants.
> —Talmud, *Ta'anit* 23a

Only after considering the holiness of the earth as a whole contrasting to the holiness of the Land of Israel in particular, and the holiness of the people contrasting to the holiness of a place, are we in a position to use one Jewish category to address the issues raised by a Process Theology of creation. Starting from within Judaism, our sources provide both possibility and pathway.

First, the Hebrew Bible asserts that a place is intrinsically holy, constituting the prime reward for good living—in this case, for *mitzvah* observance. The Rabbis presume that a place is made holy by the righteousness and piety of its inhabitants. The Land, in their view, is a necessary prerequisite for observance. People can soil the earth.

Second, humanity relates to soil in relationship. Our planet is not inert, a mute "fact," suitable only for measurement, testing, and objectification. Rather, a full human relationship to the world is one in which the earth is loved and cultivated, a partner with Jews and all other peoples in the service of God, creation, and human becoming. There is a dynamism to human-planetary interactions: our behavior allows the earth to fulfill its covenantal relationship, and our planet, in turn, provides humanity with further grounds for gratitude to God. The earth is both witness and participant in our sacred covenant (*brit*).

Third, the early Rabbis, perhaps building on the precedent established in Second Temple times, strive to articulate a notion of holiness that includes not only *Eretz Yisrael* but the rest of the world as well. Through focusing the blessings for food on agricultural produce and their subcategories, by adding liturgical petitions on behalf of the weather outside the Land of Israel, and by providing for multiple models of land sanctity, the Mishnah and the Talmud maintain a claim for the holiness of the whole earth, without relinquishing a special Jewish estimation for Israel itself. "Israel living in its Land has consequences for the entire world. When Israel lives in its Land, the entire earth can become sacred space."[1]

For Jews (and biblically centered Christians), our loyalty begins with *Eretz Yisrael*. But we are not only Jews or Christians. As both members of particular faiths *and* human beings, we also owe fealty and love to the entire planet, as well as to the particular corners we currently call home. The path of the Hebrew Bible and the early rabbinic tradition is one of expanding concentric circles, decentralizing the notion of holiness into a provisional portability that permits a relationship with the sacred anywhere and anytime. That schema sanctifies all the earth, summoning us, as seekers and as humans, to enter into a relationship of love and piety with our beleaguered planet.

The earth can either be our partner in the service of God or our prosecutor, testifying before all creation about our pettiness, self-interest, and shortsightedness. We can make of this planet a place where God's presence can comfortably dwell, so that the whole world becomes a sanctuary (*mishkan*). As always, we face a choice.

Conclusion
Clay in the Potter's Hands—
Telling the Creation Story
from the Inside

In the waning days of the kingdom of Judah, which was surrounded by enemies intending to attack and corrupted from within by a lack of will, clarity, and identity, the prophet Jeremiah addressed the people of Israel time and again, calling us back to who we are meant to be. On one occasion he says:

> Then I went down to the potter's house, and found him working at the wheel. And if the vessel he was making was spoiled, as happens to clay in the potter's hands, he would make it into another vessel, such as the potter saw fit to make. Then the word of the Holy One came to me: "O House of Israel, can I not deal with you like this potter?" says the Holy One. "Just like clay in the hand of the potter, so are you in My hands, O House of Israel." (Jeremiah 18:3–6).

These famous lines of the prophet Jeremiah make their way as a poem (*piyyut*) into the Rosh Ha-Shanah prayer book, "As clay in the hand of the potter who thickens or thins it at will, so are we in Your hand, O God of love. Recall Your covenant and show Your mercy."

In the course of this *piyyut*, we, the Jewish people, are compared to clay, to stone, to iron, to glass, to cloth, and to silver. I would argue that this *piyyut* has been misunderstood more than almost any other poetic image in the *machzor* (High Holy Day prayer book). The way most commentaries speak about it, we are completely inert and absolutely in God's control. God molds us according to absolute will, untrammeled coercive power, and we are simply the passive recipients of God's might, omniscience, total knowledge, and force.

However ubiquitous it may be, this interpretation is wrong, scientifically and religiously.

Anybody who has worked with clay knows there are things one can do with clay, and there are things the clay will tolerate. Anyone who has worked with cloth, metal, glass, or precious gems knows that the matter with which you are doing your work constrains the results you are able to achieve. The material has, if you will, its own *chokhmah*, its own wisdom. And the stuff you work with creates a partnership with the artisan. We do not like to think of our interactions like that; we like to think that when we do something we are in control. How many cooks can guarantee that a recipe turns out perfectly every time? Obviously, the dish you are making has a mind of its own, as does the oven, as do the ingredients. How much the more so, then, when it comes to living beings. If the clay has its own property that it embodies in the world uniquely, how much the more so human beings or any of God's creatures.

What this amazing poem is telling us, then, is that God kneads clay *as clay*, mindful of clay's nature, working through and with that distinctive way of being. And God works with metal appropriately for metal, mindful of its metallic nature. And God needs us and works with each of us, and all of us, in our uniqueness, as we each are. This poem does not portray oppressive domination. It is not about an all-powerful, active God and wormlike, passive human beings to be ruthlessly crushed at divine will. We call God in this very poem a "God of love." Love is when you know someone well enough that you know what it is they need to accentuate, when you know how to coax them into something truly magnificent. A great potter is not someone who crushes the clay; a great potter intuits and invites the clay into magnificent functional art. And so this poem and the liturgy we recite on one of the holiest of days are really a song about God's uncanny ability to know us and all creation from the inside, to know what we and every creature can bear and what we cannot, to know what are our strengths and what are our needs, and to urge us, to invite us, to take the next step into our own becoming, our own greatness. And to do the same for every event throughout the cosmos, for all of creation: *la-brit habet*, "look to the covenant." What is the covenant if not a relationship between two responsive individuals? If one crushes the other, that is not a *brit*; that is a *milchamah*, a war! Life is not about God attempting to conquer. Life is about God calling us and all creation into relationship.

So the message for us is very simple: we are nothing less than who we are! Each one of us—clay in God's hands—is unique and different from each and every other. It is God's greatness to recognize our uniqueness, and our frailty to forget. So we all assume that everyone is just like us, and if they are not, that they should be. But it is not true; creatures are not simply duplicates of each other. Some are clay, some are wood, some are stone, and some are precious jewels. All are worthy in their own unique way.

A Dynamic World of Novelty

Everything that comes into the world brings novelty into the world, something that has never before been seen.

Let us start with the first great novelty—fourteen billion years ago, with the world exploding into existence at the very moment of the big bang. For the first two billion years, as both the Torah and science tell us, there was light, there was energy, and there were elementary particles. The first stars probably formed a few million years after the big bang (in a period called the epoch of reionization). We are the product of that light, those quarks. Out of the big bang came only two elements: hydrogen and helium. That is all that was created at the beginning. These two elements each brought its own *chokhmah*, its own way of reacting, into the world. The initial matter was probably cold and static, but it gradually warmed through gravitational contraction until finally nuclear reactions were triggered. Those reactions heated matter. With time, the earliest stardust enriched later generations of stars. As they collided and mixed, collided and mixed and congealed, they formed intense burning fireball stars. After two billion years of darkness, the entire cosmos ignited, and there was light everywhere. The cosmos's initial expansion was at an unprecedented rate, as these stars lit up the night sky for the first time ever. And it continues to expand, although more modestly.

Then, as if that illumination were not miraculous enough, some of these stars became so overheated, so big and dense, that they collapsed in on themselves, exploding novel material out into the world: nitrogen and carbon, and all sorts of elements of complexity that had never previously existed, which were spit out into the sky and ultimately made possible you and me. We would not exist without carbon; without iron. We would not exist without these elements that were created long after the beginning of the big bang. If God's work had stopped in the first moment, we would not be here. But God's creation is a continuing creation, an unceasing creation. So round two was the explosion of the supernovae—that still give of themselves to the cosmos—donating their innards to the process that eventually led to life.

Then, more miraculous yet, billions of years later, in one of these swirling galaxies, on one of its outermost rings, is a star of just the right size—not too big and not too small—just the right density, just the right heat. Around it, a circle of dust spins around and around, and gradually the particles of exploded stardust gather into spheres, and those orbs cluster into the planets of our solar system.

On one very lucky planet, the third rock from our sun, there is pervasive thunder and lightning, but not lightning like you and I see today. The lightning of ten billion years ago is a lightning that is constant and everywhere. The entire earth is nothing but molten heat that spits up to the surface, hardens into rock, and dives back down so that—unique among the planets—the heavier elements do not remain buried in the core; they ascend to the surface and mix with the air and the planet's crust. In that lightning/water/frothy mix, life emerges. Do you know what powers our consciousness? We are packets of lightning! Our nervous systems are electrical systems. The flash of lightning that burst into life eons ago bursts inside of you at this moment. I am writing words powered by embodied lightning. And you understand me for the same reason, because this book— you can share with others—this writing is electric!

Little packets of channeled lightning start to mingle and mix, and we have been mingling and mixing every since.

And then, as if that were not miracle enough, these little packets of lightning—without prior organization or planning—they learn how to take other matter in and use it to build their own continuity. Life learns to eat. Life learns to digest life. Life learns to grow by building more life, and the miracles continue as cells learn how to convey information. (We are not the first to do it: there was instant messaging ten million years ago. That is what genetics is all about; the ability of one cell to tell another cell what to do.) And so cells master the capacity to convey information. Our ancestors get some backbone and then do something astonishing, unprecedented: they leave our mother, the ocean.

We already asserted that each of us is portable lightning, but that is not the whole story. We are also portable containers of ocean; the saline solution of our blood is closer to the content of ocean water than we might suspect. We are living, walking puddles of ocean, powered by lightning. In our bodies is the entire story of the universe's creation. We ourselves contain the energy of the big bang, the primordial lightning out of which life emerged, the salty life-giving brine of the sea, the sociability of primates—all of that millennial history is in each of us. All of creation is in each of us.

The twentieth-century French philosopher Paul Valéry says, "The universe is built on a plan, the profound symmetry of which is somehow present in the inner structure of our own intellect."[1] Our minds, our bodies, our emotions, our way of being in the world are the universe itself organized into consciousness—or the universe organizing itself and erupting into consciousness.

We have everything we need for the journey. We are already packed. In fact, the packing has been done for us!

Picture, if you will, our cousin, the bear. Picture specifically a mother bear in the dead of winter asleep in her lair, under a layer of ice and snow. Picture, nestled inside her warm body, little bear twins waiting to be born. Evolutionary cosmologist Brian Swimme and eco-theologian Thomas Berry remind us in *The Universe Story* that inside their mother's womb, those baby bears have paws that already antici-pate how salmon swim.[2] Those paws have been shaped, sculpted, and caressed by millions of years of development so that when these cubs are born, they already have the feel of salmon at the end of their paws. They have been honed over millions of years so that their fur already knows the feeling of the first snows, of autumn air turning crisp and cold, and the time to sleep. Their tongues already taste the sweetness of berries; they know what it is like to have fruit juice dripping down their chins. Those bear cubs have never yet been in the world and yet they have everything they need for the journey. And so do you.

Shaped by Our Past, Prepared for Tomorrow

In our mother's womb, we also were equipped with everything we need. God is indeed like a potter, but not a tyrant. God is a loving potter who has fashioned us across hundreds of millions of years so that the moment we come into this world we emerge social, curious, interested, connected, outraged by injustice, delighted by joy. We do not teach babies to smile at a smile; they remind us to smile! We carry in our very bodies our cosmic and evolutionary history.

Years and years ago, our ancestors decided, not with their minds but with their bodies, that human beings would have unusually large brains. This collective choice has made all the difference. Creatures with crania the size of ours must be born early. Mothers cannot carry such babies to term; the infants' heads are too big. But if our babies were going to be born early and their heads were going to be that big, then we needed a certain voluptuous wide hip among our females. And we were going to need a certain protective machismo among the men, because those women were going to get stuck holding those babies for an awful long time! Our ancient ancestors' bodies adapted, exaggerating the gender differences that existed in other primates so that men would be protective dads and women would be resilient mothers.

With those babies in our arms, we stood up so that we could scan the distance. And that standing up made all the difference. This action developed for us not just backaches but also the need and the ability to walk the long distances that we did. We walked out of Eastern Africa; we walked into the Middle East; we walked over to Asia; we hoofed it over to Europe; we even made it by way of Russia into Alaska and down into the New World. We have been walking and wandering ever since—living portable containers of ocean powered by lightning.

We Are Everything We Need

Every day is a day for us to remember that we have been given everything we need. We do not have to work *on* it or *for* it; it is already in us. It *is* us. We have it.

The prophet Jeremiah, articulating God's Word, says to us, "Before I formed you in the belly, I knew you; and before you came forth out of the womb I sanctified you" (Jeremiah 1:5). We have been sanctified by God over billions of years, through miracle upon miracle; by fortuitous and unlikely chance that has led to this moment, right now. Astonishing! The reasonable response to the many gifts we have been given through creation is to exult in joy; to celebrate the crescendo of the cosmos that is us, that pulses through us; to celebrate it in each other, in who we have become, in what our promises are.

We have everything we need. We are in the hands of a Potter who seeks to understand us well enough to let us become the glorious pottery we actually are, a creation of magnificent diversity, emergent mindfulness, and one truly super nature!

Acknowledgments

This book offers a Creation Theology from a Jewish perspective, integrating science and religion through the lens of Process Thought.

As with any book, there are many people to thank:

Thanks to my friend Stuart M. Matlins, visionary founder and publisher of Jewish Lights; Emily Wichland, editor extraordinaire who has now helped me craft and hone three books into their best possible versions; Debra Hirsch Corman, masterful copy editor; Leah Brewer, skilled publicist; and the talented people at Jewish Lights, who accepted an unfinished manuscript and produced a beautiful and significantly better book.

While writing this book, it has been my delight to serve as the Abner and Roslyn Goldstein Dean of the Ziegler School of Rabbinic Studies and vice president of American Jewish University in Los Angeles, California. I am reminded daily of the blessing of working with an outstanding group of people: students, faculty, administration, and lay leaders. My deepest thanks go to the university's president, Dr. Robert Wexler, who is both mentor and friend; to Rabbi Cheryl Peretz, Rabbi Ephraim Pelcovits, and Reb Mimi Feigelson— partners in building a world-class rabbinical school in the context of holiness, goodness, and friendship; to Rabbi Aaron Alexander, for a decade associate dean for the Ziegler School and a dear friend to this day; to Rabbi Adam Greenwald, partner in creating a preeminent center of Jewish outreach; to the superb members of the faculty; and to my beloved students—rabbis and soon-to-be rabbis. It is a privilege and a joy to work at such a wonderful *makom Torah*.

My continuing thanks and affection also go to the Jewish Theological Seminary, where I was ordained as a rabbi and where I still cherish friendships and many close ties, and to the Hebrew Union College–Jewish Institute of Religion, where I was granted the privilege of doctoral studies under the scholarly and humane supervision of my teacher and friend Rabbi David Ellenson.

My beloved family has provided a constant backdrop of love and support. I am deeply grateful to my mother, Barbara Friedman Artson, and her companion, Richard Lichtman; my father, David Artson, and his wife, Jeanne; my sister and sister-in-law, Tracy and Dawn Osterweil-Artson; my niece, Sydney, and my nephew, Benjamin; my brother, Matthew Artson; my brother and sister-in-law, Danny and Shirli Shavit, and my nephews and niece, Alon, Roy, and Maya; and Grace Mayeda, my beloved childhood nanny.

I am happy to be able to dedicate this book about creation to those loving people who were the channels of creation in my own life: my parents and grandparents. I perch on their shoulders and thrive in their embrace.

I have been privileged to have many wonderful rabbis and spiritual guides enrich my life—too many to list—and I am grateful to each and every one of them.

My children, Jacob and Shira, fill my life with profound joy and purpose. They provide the greatest evidence of continuing creation as they continue to blossom into people of such dignity, grace, and generosity of spirit. It is a joy to see them shine.

My beloved wife, Elana, is my partner in all of life's moments and in every creative moment I have touched. She inspires with the way her resilient goodness strengthens those around her, and her keen access to life's reservoirs of vision and strength have made our family possible and our marriage a joyous blessing.

Acharon acharon chaviv—I am grateful beyond words to the Holy Blessing One. You create the world anew each moment, and You grace each and every one of us with the capacity to partner in the unfolding of a world of greater experience, love, compassion, and justice. You are the source of light and creativity; in Your light we see light and refract it back out into Your glorious world.

My blessing for us all is that we open ourselves to join in this pageant of creation, dancing the ancient rhythm of life celebrating itself in the service of its Maker, so that all humans feel the familial support of every other person, so that we each reverberate to the worthy achievements and respond to alleviate the suffering of our brothers and sisters throughout the human family, and that we humans extend our sense of shared destiny and awe to link us to our nonhuman cousins throughout the biosphere and ground us in a cosmos that is wondrous beyond all imagining. Then we shall know true contentment. And then God's name shall be truly One.

Tam Ve-nishlam Shevach Le-El Borei Olam.

Notes

Introduction

1. "In whose goodness renews creation every day constantly," from the weekday morning prayer book. Another variant of this phrase, "who renews every day the work of creation," is found in *Midrash Psalms* 96:1 and elsewhere.
2. Alfred North Whitehead, *Process and Reality: An Essay in Cosmology*, corrected ed., ed. David Ray Griffin and Donald W. Sherburne (New York: Free Press, 1978), 21.

Part I

1. Laboratory journal entry #10,040 (March 19, 1849); published in *The Life and Letters of Faraday*, vol. 2, ed. Henry Bence Jones (London: Longmans, Green, and Co., 1870), 253.

Chapter 1

1. Moses Maimonides, *The Guide for the Perplexed*, trans. Shlomo Pines (Chicago: University of Chicago, 1963), 9.
2. Evelyn Fox Keller, *Making Sense of Life: Explaining Biological Development with Models, Metaphors and Machines* (Cambridge, MA: Harvard University Press, 2002).
3. Ian Barbour, *Religion and Science: Historical and Contemporary Issues* (San Francisco: HarperSanFrancisco, 1997), 77–106.
4. For a comprehensive reflection on this human endeavor to integrate and explain, see Nelson Goodman, *Ways of Worldmaking* (Indianapolis: Hackett, 1988).

Chapter 2

1. John Wheeler, quoted in Marcelo Gleiser, *The Dancing Universe: From Creation Myths to the Big Bang* (New York: Plume Books, 1998), 257.
2. Ian Barbour, *Religion and Science: Historical and Contemporary Issues* (San Francisco: HarperSanFrancisco, 1997), 180.
3. This material is explained clearly and masterfully in Nancy Ellen Abrams and Joel R. Primack, *The New Universe and the Human Future* (New Haven, CT: Yale University Press, 2011).
4. For greater background, see Marcelo Gleiser, chap. 8, "Of Things Small," in *The Dancing Universe: From Creation Myths to the Big Bang* (New York: Plume Books, 1997); John Polkinghorne, *Quantum Theory: A Very Short Introduction* (Oxford: Oxford University Press, 2002).
5. The Pauli exclusion principle states that no two identical fermions may occupy the same quantum state simultaneously. For electrons in a single atom, it states that no two electrons can have the same four quantum numbers. All material particles exhibit space-occupying behavior.
6. James P. Crutchfield, Doyne Farmer, Norman H. Packard, and Robert Shaw, "Chaos," *Scientific American* 255, no. 6 (December 1986): 38.
7. Paul Davies, *The Cosmic Blueprint: New Discoveries in Nature's Creative Ability to Order the Universe* (Philadelphia: Templeton Foundation Press, 2004), xvi.

Chapter 3

1. See, for example, John R. Searle, *Mind: A Brief Introduction* (Oxford: Oxford University Press, 2005).
2. Stephen Jay Gould, "The Exaptive Excellence of Spandrels as a Term and Prototype," *Proceedings of the National Academy of Sciences USA* 94 (September 1997): 10750–55.

Chapter 4

1. See Lee Smolin, *The Life of the Cosmos* (New York: Oxford University Press, 1997).
2. Paul Davies, in Niel Henrik Gregersen, *From Complexity to Life: On the Emergence of Life and Meaning* (Oxford: Oxford University Press, 2003), 10.
3. Martin Rees, *Just Six Numbers: The Deep Forces That Shape the Universe* (New York: Basic Books, 2000), 2–3. Additional extraordinary examples of fine-tuning include the smoothness of the universe, the early inflation, the masses of superheavy particles, the electron-proton mass difference, and the nature of carbon, to name a few.

4. Michael J. Denton collates a similar list in the realm of biochemistry and biology in *Nature's Destiny: How the Laws of Biology Reveal Purpose in the Universe* (New York: Free Press, 1998).

5. See John D. Barrow and Frank J. Tipler, *The Anthropic Cosmological Principle* (Oxford: Oxford University Press, 1988); and Paul Davies, *God and the New Physics* (New York: Simon & Schuster, 1983).

6. John Leslie, "The Anthropic Principle Today," in *Modern Cosmology & Philosophy*, ed. John Leslie (New York: Prometheus Books, 1998), 290.

7. John Wheeler called this a participatory anthropic principle (PAP) and describes it as "symbolic representation of the Universe as a self-excited system brought into being by 'self-reference.' The universe gives birth to communicating participators. Communicating participators give meaning to the universe.... With such a concept goes the endless series of receding reflections one sees in a pair of facing mirrors." See John Archibald Wheeler in *Quantum Gravity*, ed. C. J. Isham, P. Penrose, and D. W. Sciama (Oxford: Clarendon Press, 1975), 564–565.

8. Such reflections invite, indeed encourage, the use of personal metaphors for the Divine.

9. The term "value concept" comes from Max Kadushin, indicating terms that are simultaneously values *and* concepts.

10. Paul Davies, "Teleology without Teleology: Purpose through Emergent Complexity," in *In Whom We Live and Move and Have Our Being: Panentheistic Reflections on God's Presence in a Scientific World*, ed. Philip Clayton and Arthur Peacocke (Grand Rapids, MI: William B. Eerdmans, 2004), 95.

11. Philip Clayton, *Mind & Emergence: From Quantum to Consciousness* (Oxford: Oxford University Press, 2004), 5; Clayton and Davies, *The Re-Emergence of Emergence: The Emergentist Hypothesis from Science to Religion* (New York: Oxford University Press, 2006), 308. Clayton credits this insight to William C. Wimsatt, "The Ontology of Complex Systems: Levels of Organization, Perspectives, and Causal Thickets," *Canadian Journal of Philosophy*, 24, suppl. 1 (1994): 207–274.

12. It should be noted that freedom, complexity, and novelty do not always produce events we perceive as positive. Typhoons, draught, and plague all reflect freedom, complexity, and novelty. What is new and relational need not be cheery and beneficial from our perspective and often is not.

Chapter 5

1. Pierre Simon LaPlace, *Philosophical Essays on Probabilities*, trans. Frederick Wilson Truscott and Frederick Lincoln Emory (New York: Cosimo Books, 2007), 4.

2. See Brian Greene, *The Elegant Universe: Superstrings, Hidden Dimensions, and the Quest for the Ultimate Theory* (New York: Vintage Books, 2000), for an eloquent and passionate presentation of this unflagging search.

3. And in chapter 1 of Bradley Shavit Artson, *God of Becoming and Relationship: The Dynamic Nature of Process Theology* (Woodstock, VT: Jewish Lights, 2013).

4. In fairness, some recent descriptions of natural laws do acknowledge that the law is a descriptive tool, a conceptual generalization of concrete phenomena, not an objective reality of its own. For example, "in science, a law is a descriptive principle of nature that holds in all circumstances covered by the wording of the law" (John Daintith and Elizabeth Martin, *A Dictionary of Science* [Oxford: Oxford University Press, 2005], 464); or "[in logic], a stated regularity in the relations or order of phenomena in the world that holds, under a stipulated set of conditions, either universally or in a stated proportion of instances" (*Encyclopedia Britannica Online*, s.v. "Nature, law of," July 6, 2009, www.britannica.com/topic/law-of-nature).

5. "Secondary and approximate" remains quite significant. Newtonian physics, for example, is also secondary and approximate, yet we continue to rely on it for daily life and for most mechanics.

6. The astute reader will reverberate echoes of Franz Rosenzweig. See "The New Thinking," in *Philosophical and Theological Writings*, ed. Paul. W. Franks and Michael L. Morgan (Indianapolis: Hackett, 2000), also found in *Franz Rosenzweig's "The New Thinking,"* ed. Alan Udoff and Barbara E. Galli (Syracuse, NY: Syracuse University Press, 1999).

7. See William R. Stroeger, S.J., "Contemporary Physics and the Ontological Status of the Laws of Nature," in *Quantum Cosmology and The Laws of Nature: Scientific Perspectives on Divine Action*, ed. Robert John Russell, Nancey Murphy, and C. J. Isham (Notre Dame, IN: Notre Dame Press, 1999), 207–231.

8. Louis Jacobs, "Jewish Cosmology," in *Ancient Cosmologies*, ed. Carmen Blacker and Michael Loewe (London: George Allen & Unwin Ltd, 1975), 29. A page later, he observes that the concept of universal law "is anachronistic when applied to the thought of the Rabbis" (p. 30).

9. J. A. Wheeler, in *Problems in Theoretical Physics*, ed. A. Giovanni, F. Mancini, and M. Marino (Salerno: University of Salerno Press, 1984).

10. Rolf Landauer, "Computation and Physics: Wheeler's Meaning Circuit," *Foundations of Physics* 16, no. 6 (1986): 551–564.

11. A controversial but evocative expression of this sentiment is Mach's principle, which states, "The inertia of any particular matter is attributable to the interaction between that piece of matter and the rest of the universe"; John Daintith, *Oxford Dictionary of Physics* (Oxford: Oxford University Press, 2005), 297. Mach's insight, contested to this

day, had an important impact on Einstein's formulation of general relativity.

Chapter 6

1. Saadia Gaon, *The Book of Beliefs and Opinions*, trans. Samuel Rosenblatt (New Haven, CT: Yale University Press, 1948), 96.
2. Whitehead, *Process and Reality*, 343.
3. The idea for the comma and the term comes from Sallie McFague, *Super, Natural Christians: How We Should Love Nature* (Minneapolis: Augsburg Fortress, 2000).
4. Hans Jonas, *Mortality and Morality: A Search for the Good after Auschwitz* (Evanston, IL: Northwestern University Press, 1996), 63.
5. Milton Steinberg, *A Believing Jew: The Selected Writings of Milton Steinberg* (New York: Harcourt, Brace, 1951), 19.
6. Jonas, *Mortality and Morality*, 77.
7. Steinberg, *A Believing Jew*, 19.
8. Coco Ballantyne, "Planning of the Apes," *Scientific American*, May 2009, 27.
9. Irene Pepperberg, *From Alex & Me: How a Scientist and a Parrot Discovered a Hidden World of Animal Intelligence—and Formed a Deep Bond in the Process* (New York: HarperCollins, 2008), quoted in *Discover Magazine*, February 2009, 77.
10. Emily Anthes, "Avian Cooperation: Rooks Work Together to Solve Puzzle for Food," *Scientific American*, August/September 2008, 8.
11. Christof Koch, "What Is It Like to Be a Bee?," *Scientific American*, January 14, 2009, 18–19.
12. Tetsu Saigusa et al., "Amoebae Anticipate Periodic Events," *Physical Review Letters* 100, no. 1 (January 11, 2008).
13. Jonas, *Mortality and Morality*, 69.

Chapter 7

1. Maimonides, "Eight Chapters," in *A Maimonides Reader*, ed. Isadore Twersky (West Orange, NJ: Behrman House, 1972), 380.
2. Maimonides, *Mishneh Torah, Teshuvah* 5:5.
3. In fairness to Maimonides, despite the considerable theological pressure to do so from dogmatic Muslim and other Jewish thinkers, he refused to back down from his insistence on human free will and autonomy. As Alexander Altmann affirms, "Maimonides' theological writings distinctly affirm man's absolute freedom of will." Alexander Altmann, "Religion of the Thinkers: Free Will and Predestination in Saadia, Bahya, and Maimonides," *Religion in a Religious Age*, ed. S. D. Goitein (Cambridge, MA: Association for Jewish Studies, 1974), 45.

Maimonides extends that volitional freedom to animals, as does Rav Saadia.

4. Philip Clayton, *Adventures in the Spirit: God, World, Divine Action* (Minneapolis: Fortress Press, 2008), 179.

5. See, for example, John Conway and Simon Kochen, "The Free Will Theorem," *Foundations of Physics* 36 (2006): 1441–1473.

6. Significantly, even those philosophers and physicists who are committed to a metaphysics of determinism must conduct their lives as though there is free will and choice. They assert their own agency, and they rear their children (and hold accountable their students) to take responsibility, to plan ahead, to choose wisely, and to persevere. The gap between their intellectual framework (determinism) and the way they choose reality in their lives is a telling critique of their own metaphysical supposition.

7. William R. Stroeger, S.J., "The Immanent Directionality of the Evolutionary Process, and Its Relationship to Teleology," *Evolutionary and Molecular Biology: Scientific Perspectives on Divine Action* (Notre Dame: University of Notre Dame Press, 1998), 163–190; and Jeffrey P. Schloss, "Divine Providence and the Question of Evolutionary Directionality," in *Back to Darwin: A Richer Account of Evolution*, ed. John B. Cobb, Jr. (Grand Rapids, MI: William B. Eerdmans, 2008), 330–350.

8. Abraham Joshua Heschel, *God in Search of Man* (New York: Octagon Books, 1977), 412.

9. Ibid., 409.

10. *Tanchuma, Pekudei* 3.

11. Other urges—lust, hunger, rage, despair, greed, and the like—are not the lure of God, but the addiction of *tohu va-vohu*, the potent, distracting, destructive pull of chaos.

12. Rabbi Nachman of Breslov, *Likkutei MoHaRan*, 277.

13. Jonas, *Mortality and Morality*, 70.

14. Ibid., 61.

15. Ibid., 62. See also Hans Jonas, *The Phenomenon of Life: Toward a Philosophical Biology* (Evanston, IL: Northwestern University Press, 2001), 38–58.

16. Alfred North Whitehead, *Adventures of Ideas* (New York: Free Press, 1967), 296.

17. Whitehead, *Process and Reality*, 351.

Chapter 8

1. This section relies heavily on the brilliant and captivating work of Joel R. Primack and Nancy Ellen Abrams, *The View from the Center of the Universe: Discovering Our Extraordinary Place in the Cosmos* (New York: Riverhead Books, 2006).

2. For a wealth of background information and a range of translations, see Lawrence A. Hoffman and David Arnow, eds., *My People's Passover Haggadah: Traditional Texts, Modern Commentaries* (Woodstock, VT: Jewish Lights, 2008); Joshua Kulp and David Golinkin, *The Schechter Haggadah: Art, History and Commentary* (Jerusalem: Schechter Institute of Jewish Studies, 2009), 50–54, 234–235; and Joseph Tabory, *JPS Commentary on the Haggadah: Historical Introduction, Translation, and Commentary* (Philadelphia: Jewish Publication Society, 2008), 45–46, 97–99.
3. This hypothesis is untestable in principle and eludes verification or falsification. It remains quite controversial, even among scientists.
4. Alan Dressler, *Voyage to the Great Attractor: Exploring Intergalactic Space* (New York: Knopf, 1994), 335.
5. Gerald M. Edelman, *Second Nature: Brain Science and Human Knowledge* (New Haven, CT: Yale University Press, 2006), 18.

Chapter 9

1. It is often noted homiletically that each of the volumes of the Talmud begins on page 2, to indicate that there is no place for an absolute beginning—every page presumes familiarity with the entirety of Talmud. Lacking *the* beginning, in Talmud learning, one must simply dive in.
2. Talmud, *Nedarim* 3a, *Yevamot* 71a, *Avodah Zarah* 27a, *Keritot* 11a.
3. Jon D. Levenson, *Creation and the Persistence of Evil: The Jewish Drama of Divine Omnipotence* (San Francisco: Harper & Row, 1988), 12.
4. For an extended reflection, see Catherine Keller, *Face of the Deep: A Theology of Becoming* (New York: Routledge, 2003).
5. Catherine Keller, *On the Mystery: Discerning God in Process* (Minneapolis: Fortress Press, 2008), 50–51. This entire section is swimming in Keller's waters. While the entire book owes a great deal to her thoughts and words, it is especially true in this section, which I gratefully acknowledge.
6. Saadia Gaon, *The Book of Beliefs and Opinions*, trans. Samuel Rosenblatt (New Haven, CT: Yale University Press, 1948), 64.
7. Ibid., 343.
8. The term is Catherine Keller's, *On the Mystery*, 58.
9. Keller, *On the Mystery*, 48; and *Face of the Deep*, xix.
10. Talmud, *Chagigah* 15a; *Midrash Psalms* 93:5. See also Deuteronomy 32:11, where the same term describes an eagle hovering over his eaglets.
11. The author of this pithy doublet is the journalist Peter Finley Dunne.

12. Nahum M. Sarna, *The JPS Torah Commentary: Genesis* (Philadelphia: Jewish Publication Society, 1989), 7. Indeed, noted Bible scholar Gerhard von Rad identifies *merachefet* as "vibrate!"; see *Genesis: A Commentary* (Philadelphia: Westminster John Knox Press, 1972), 49.
13. Brian Greene, *Elegant Universe: Superstrings, Hidden Dimensions, and the Quest for the Ultimate Theory* (New York: Norton, 1999), 135.

Chapter 10

1. C. J. S. Clarke, "Process as a Primitive Physical Category," in *The Study of Time*, vol. 7, ed. J. T. Fraser and L. Rowell (Madison, CT: International University Press, 1993), 67.
2. Sacha Stern, *Time and Process in Ancient Judaism* (Oxford: Littman Library of Jewish Civilization, 2003), 124.
3. Ibid., p. 2.
4. On the need to liberate our thinking from the dominant grip of this Neo-Platonic system, see Artson, *God of Becoming and Relationship*, 3–8.
5. *Turei Zahav, Orach Chayim* 545:13
6. Abraham ibn Ezra, *Yesod Mora Ve-Sod Ha-Torah, The Secret of the Torah: A Translation*, trans. H. Norman Strickman (Northvale, NJ: Jason Aronson, 1995), 19.
7. Gershom Scholem, "Education for Judaism," in *On the Possibility of Jewish Mysticism in Our Time* (Philadelphia: Jewish Publication Society, 1997), 84.

Chapter 11

1. Saadia Gaon, *The Book of Beliefs and Opinions*, 101.
2. That this process is not exclusively benign is clear from the extravagance of the evolutionary history of the cosmos and life, as well as from rabbinic wisdom. Consider the Talmudic debates about whether it would have been better for humanity not to have been created, with the Rabbis ultimately agreeing that it would have been better for humanity had we not! (Talmud, *Eruvin* 13b).
3. Maimonides, "Eight Chapters," 384. It should be noted that Rambam's ethical pedagogy owes its origin to Aristotle as well as to Torah. In the realm of moral development and education, as well as in Aristotle's insistence on empirical research as the primary way to explore reality, I am also happy to acknowledge again my debt to the peripatetic philosopher.
4. Maimonides, *Guide of the Perplexed* (Chicago: University of Chicago Press, 1964), 3:13, p. 452.

Chapter 12

1. See Eugene C. Hargrove, *Foundations of Environmental Ethics* (Englewood Cliffs, NJ: Prentice Hall, 1989), 14–45.
2. René Descartes, *Discourse on Method and Meditations* (Indianapolis: Bobbs-Merrill, 1960), part 6.
3. Cited in Tom Regan and Peter Singer, eds., *Animal Rights and Human Obligations* (Englewood Cliffs, NJ: Prentice-Hall, 1976), 66.
4. Heschel, *God in Search of Man*, 34.
5. See James Lovelock, *The Ages of Gaia: A Biography of Our Living Earth* (New York: Bantam Books, 1988).
6. Aldo Leopold, *A Sand County Almanac and Sketches Here and There* (New York: Oxford University Press, 1987), 129.
7. The biologist J. B. S. Haldane, noting that beetles have inhabited the earth for 250 million years, comprising at least 500,000 species (a quarter of all known animal species), was said to have quipped, "I have learned that God has an inordinate fondness for beetles." Cited in Jay McDaniel, "A Process Approach to Ecology," in *Handbook of Process Theology*, ed. Jay McDaniel and Donna Bowman (St. Louis, MO: Chalice Press, 2006), 232.
8. See Robin Attfield, *The Ethics of Environmental Concern* (Athens, GA: University of Georgia Press, 1991), 34–51.
9. Jeremy Rifkin, *Declaration of a Heretic* (Boston: Routledge and Kegan Paul, 1985), 108.
10. The biblically attuned reader will note that this is the first mention of economic justice, surprising in a theology that posits fidelity to biblical and rabbinic traditions, with their insistence on the rights of the widow, the orphan, the poor, and the stranger. A related omission is any consideration of political power and sovereignty. These are certainly priorities that any embodied Process Theology must address, and I hope to do so in subsequent volumes exploring revelation and redemption.

Chapter 13

1. See Jeremy Benstein, *The Way Into Judaism and the Environment* (Woodstock, VT: Jewish Lights, 2008); Martin D. Yaffe, ed., *Judaism and Environmental Ethics: A Reader* (Lanham, MD: Lexington Books, 2001); and Hava Tirosh-Samuelson, ed., *Judaism and Ecology: Created World and Revealed Word* (New York: Cassell, 2007).
2. See Jean Holm and John Bowker, eds., *Attitudes to Nature* (London: Pinter, 1994); and Noel J. Brown and Pierre Quiblier, eds., *Ethics & Agenda 21: Moral Implications of a Global Consensus* (New York: United Nations Publications, 1994).

3. Nowhere is this fruitful tension more evident than in balancing the commandment of *peru u-revu*, to be fruitful and multiply, with the obligation to guard creation. The explosion of human numbers threatens the ability of the biosphere to continue to maintain balance. How do we care for the continuation of all living things and still fulfill our obligation to reproduce? One answer might be to seek ways in which human reproduction does not threaten biodiversity, perhaps by limiting our children to two per couple, perhaps by learning to live within certain spaces already occupied by humans, perhaps more boldly by declaring that *mitzvah* to reproduce pertains not to individuals but to humanity as a species—in which case it is fulfilled and no longer binding. Perhaps now we can shift our attention to the *mitzvah* of *giddel banim*, of raising children—our own (biological or adopted) and those of our neighbors, family, and community.

4. Most famously, Lynn White Jr., "The Historical Roots of Our Ecological Crisis," *Science* 155 (March 10, 1967): 1203–1207; and Arnold Toynbee, "The Religious Background of the Present Environmental Crisis," *International Journal of Environmental Studies* 3 (1972): 141–146.

5. *Ba'al Ha-Turim, Bereishit* 1:1. Found in *Perush Ha-Rosh* to Exodus 20:1 and *Tikkunei Zohar* 13a [72a].

6. W. Godfrey-Smith, "The Value of Wilderness," *Environmental Ethics* 1, no. 4 (Winter 1979): 311.

7. Charles Birth and John B. Cobb Jr., *The Liberation of Life: From the Cell to the Community* (Denton, OH: Environmental Ethics Books, 1990), 150.

8. Larry L. Rasmussen, *Earth Community, Earth Ethics* (Maryknoll, NY: Orbis Books, 1996), 236.

9. Indeed, this is one rabbinic passage that cites the notion of partnership in creation as a heresy: "Adam was created on the eve of the Sabbath, why? Lest the *minim*/heretics say: The Holy Blessing One has a partner in the work of creation." Humanity's emergence last in the order of creation (which corresponds to how recently *Homo sapiens* emerged in the evolutionary tale) is a caution against heresy and excessive pride, an invitation to immediate service ("that they might immediately enter upon the fulfillment of a commandment"), and celebration of creation ("that they might straightway go in to the banquet"). Another such passage is found in *Midrash Psalms* 24:4.

10. *Tanna De-Vei Eliyahu Rabbah* 2.

11. That the Rabbis (as with the ancients in general) assumed that the species alive in their time were the same species that had always existed is a significant discrepancy from current opinion. What we do continue to share with them is a value placed on the preservation of existent species and life's diversity.

12. See Jehuda Feliks, *"Kilayim,"* in *Encyclopaedia Judaica* (New York: Macmillan, 1971), 10:999–1001.

13. Ramban to Leviticus 19:19.

14. *Sefer Ha-Chinnukh* #515.

15. Ramban to Deuteronomy 22:6.

16. *Sefer Ha-Chinnukh* #294.

17. David Kraemer, *Learn Torah With ...* (Los Angeles: Torah Aura, 1995).

18. Rabbi Nachman of Breslov, *Likkutei MoHaRan*, 306.

19. Rabbi Abraham Isaac Kook, *Orot Ha-Kodesh* 2:444.

Chapter 14

1. An earlier version of this chapter appeared in *Conservative Judaism* as "Embracing Death, Embracing the World: Our Alienation from Death and Creation," *Conservative Judaism* 48, no. 2 (Winter 1996): 49–54. Reprinted with permission.

2. Abraham ibn Ezra, translated and adapted by Rabbi Sidney Greenberg and Rabbi Jonathan D. Levine, cited in *A Garden of Choice Fruits: 200 Classic Jewish Quotes on Human Beings and the Environment*, ed. David E. Stein (Wyncote, PA: Shomrei Adamah, 1991), 66. Reprinted with permission.

3. *Shulchan Arukh, Yoreh De'ah* 339:4; *Ma'avar Yavok* 2:15.

4. *Sefer Hasidim* 650; Jerusalem Talmud, *Shabbat* 23:5. See also Yekutiel Yehudah Greenwald, *Kol Bo Al Avelut* (New York: Feldheim, n.d.), chap. 7.

5. Deuteronomy 23; Talmud, *Sanhedrin* 46b.

6. *Mishnah Sanhedrin* 6:5; Talmud, *Mo'ed Katan* 27b.

7. Genesis 50:26; *Mishnah Eduyot* 5:6; Jerusalem Talmud, *Kilayim* 9:4.

8. *Mishnah Pe'ah* 1:1; Talmud, *Berakhot* 18a; Maimonides, *Mishneh Torah, Hilkhot Avel* 14:1.

9. *Shulchan Arukh, Yoreh De'ah* 375:1; *Ma'avar Yavok*, chap. 18.

10. See *Sefer Poked Ikkarim*, 6, *"Hineh"*; and *Sefer Divrei Sofrim, Likkutei Amarim*, 16, *"Ve-sheni."*

11. *Midrash Proverbs* 14; translation taken from Burton L. Visotzky, *The Midrash on Proverbs* (New Haven, CT: Yale University Press, 1992), 74. See also Talmud, *Berakhot* 48b and *Shabbat* 30a, in which God conveys the same grave truth to King David.

12. The saying is that of Rabbi Elazar Ha-Kappar.

13. See "The Mandate to Heal," in David M. Feldman, *Health and Medicine in the Jewish Tradition* (New York: Crossroad, 1986).

14. Hans Jonas, "Contemporary Problems in Ethics from a Jewish Perspective," *Judaism and Environmental Ethics: A Reader*, ed. Martin D. Yaffe (Lanham, MD: Lexington Books, 2001), 263.

Part V

1. An earlier version of this section was published in *Conservative Judaism* 44 (1991–1992): 25–35; and in *Judaism and Environmental Ethics: A Reader*, ed. Martin D. Yaffe (Lanham, MD: Lexington Books, 2001), 161–171.
2. This consideration of a Jewish relationship with the Land of Israel and the rest of the lands of the earth is from the perspective of creation. In subsequent volumes I intend to revisit this topic from the perspectives of revelation and redemption, which will lead to explorations of more contemporary debates on Zionism, Judaism and democracy, other people's rights in Israel and Palestine, among others.

Chapter 15

1. For an extensive discussion of the importance of place and the sanctity of a specific location in Judaism, see Jonathan Z. Smith, *To Take Place: Toward Theory in Ritual* (Chicago: University of Chicago Press, 1987).
2. See T. H. Gaster, "Earth," in *Interpreter's Dictionary of the Bible* [*IDB*] (Nashville, TN: Abingdon Press, 1962), 2:2–3.
3. *Midrash Ha-Gadol, Bereishit*; and E. A. Speiser, *The Anchor Bible: Genesis* (New York: Doubleday, 1982), 16n5.
4. See also Amos 5:8; Psalms 19:2, 24:1, 105:44–45.
5. See S. Talmon, "Wilderness," *IDB Supplement* (Nashville, TN: Abingdon Press, 1984), 946–948; and Exodus 4:27, 33:12; Deuteronomy 1:31; 1 Kings 19:4–8; Hosea 2:16–17; Isaiah 41:18–20; Jeremiah 2:2, 31:2–3.
6. "Unclean" and "clean" carry a hygienic connotation to most English speakers that is not what *tamei* and *tahor* intend. Those ritual terms resist precise English translation: "purity/impurity" is another frequent rendering.
7. See also Ezekiel 4:13.
8. See also Isaiah 52:11.
9. Harry Orlinsky, "The Biblical Conquest of the Land of Israel," in *The Land of Israel: Jewish Perspectives*, ed. Lawrence A. Hoffman (Notre Dame, IN: University of Notre Dame Press, 1986), 53. This observation was made in *Mekhilta, Piska* 1: "Before the Land had been especially chosen, all lands were suitable for divine revelation; after the Land had been chosen, all other lands were eliminated."
10. Rashi understood this paradox and comments on it. See his first comment to Genesis 1:1, on *"Bereishit."*
11. This reasoning is made explicit in the Talmud (*Sanhedrin* 39a): "The Holy Blessing One said to the children of Israel, 'Sow for six years and

leave the land at rest for the seventh year, so that you may know the land is Mine.'"

12. Leviticus 19:9–10; Deuteronomy 24:19–21; *Mishnah Pe'ah*.

13. Leviticus 19:23–25; *Mishnah Orlah*.

14. Exodus 29:27; Numbers 15:18–19; *Mishnah Terumot*.

15. Exodus 23:19; Deuteronomy 26:10–11; *Mishnah Bikkurim*.

16. For a few examples, see Leviticus 18:24–30, 20:22–26; Numbers 35:34; Deuteronomy 4:40, 21:6–9; Psalm 106:38–46.

17. See, e.g., Isaiah 1:2, 41:1, 49:1.

18. Monford Harris, "Ecology: A Covenantal Approach," *CCAR Journal* 23 (Summer 1976): 101–108.

19. W. D. Davies, *The Territorial Dimension of Judaism* (Berkeley, CA: University of California Press, 1982), 134–135.

20. Charles Primus, "The Borders of Judaism: The Land of Israel in Early Rabbinic Judaism," in *The Land of Israel: Jewish Perspectives*, ed. Lawrence A. Hoffman (Notre Dame, IN: University of Notre Dame Press, 1986), 102.

21. *Mishnah Orlah* 3:9; *Tosefta Terumah* 2:13; *Tosefta Orlah* 1:8; *Tosefta Kiddushin* 1:9–10, 1:12.

22. See *Mishnah Mikva'ot* 8:1.

23. *Mishnah Oholot* 2:3, 17:5, 18:6–7; *Mishnah Tohorot* 4:5, 5:1; *Mishnah Nazir* 3:6, 7:3; *Tosefta Mikva'ot* 6:1; *Tosefta Oholot* 17:7–18:11.

24. *Mishnah Shevi'it* 5:7; *Tosefta Challah* 2:6; *Tosefta Terumah* 4:13.

25. Richard S. Sarason, "The Significance of the Land of Israel in the Mishnah," in *The Land of Israel: Jewish Perspectives*, ed. Lawrence A. Hoffman (Notre Dame, IN: University of Notre Dame Press, 1986), 123.

26. Primus, "Borders of Judaism," 107.

27. James Sanders argues, in *Torah and Canon* (Eugene, OR: Wipf and Stock, 2005) that this transformation was engineered long before the Rabbis, during the First Babylonian Exile. That argument has merit but does not affect the substance of my position, which is that the Judaisms of the First Temple period reflected a religion that presupposed living in the Land of Israel and that later Judaisms were made portable.

28. See also *Mishnah Keilim* 1:6: "There are ten degrees of holiness. The Land of Israel is holier than any other land. Wherein lies its holiness? In that from it they may bring the *omer*, the first fruits, and the two loaves, which they may not bring from any other land." That same exclusive prerogative forms the principal subject of *Mishnah Challah* 4:1–11.

29. Even prophecy, which is linked in scripture to the Land of Israel, was a possibility in other lands as well. The *Mekhilta*, *Piska* 1, makes note of this at least three times.

30. See Arnold A. Lasker and Daniel J. Lasker, "The Strange Case of December 4: A Liturgical Problem," *Conservative Judaism* 38 (1985):

91–96; and "The Jewish Prayer for Rain in Babylonia," *Journal for the Study of Judaism* (June 1984): 123–144.

31. For the history of the Ben Meir calendar controversy, see Henry Malter, *Life and Works of Saadia Gaon* (Philadelphia: Jewish Publication Society, 1921).

32. Jacob Neusner, "Map without Territory: Mishnah's System of Sacrifice and Sanctuary," *History of Religions* 19 (1979): 125.

Chapter 16

1. The discussion that follows is based on the work of Lawrence Hoffman, particularly his "Introduction: Land of Blessing and Blessings of Land," in *The Land of Israel: A Jewish Perspective* (Notre Dame, IN: University of Notre Dame Press, 1986), 1–23. Hoffman's interest is primarily what the structure of blessings reveals about rabbinic attitudes toward the Land of Israel. Our interest in this case is to examine what that same structure reveals about rabbinic attitudes toward the earth in general.

2. Clifford Geertz, *The Interpretation of Cultures* (New York: Basic Books, 1970), 10.

3. Wayne Meeks, *The First Urban Christians: The Social World of the Apostle Paul* (New Haven, CT: Yale University Press, 1983), 141.

4. Hoffman, "Introduction: Land of Blessing and Blessings of Land."

5. A series of such quotations continues on the following side (35b), calling such a practice "robbery" against God and the Jewish people. See also *Tosafot Berakhot* 4:1.

6. Hoffman, "Introduction: Land of Blessing and Blessings of Land," 15.

Chapter 17

1. Primus, "Borders of Judaism," 106.

Conclusion

1. In Jefferson Hane Weaver, *The World of Physics* (New York: Simon & Schuster, 1987), 2:521.

2. Brian Swimme and Thomas Berry, *The Universe Story: From the Primordial Flaring Forth to the Ecozoic Era—A Celebration of the Unfolding of the Cosmos* (New York: HarperOne, 1992).

Suggestions for Further Reading

Process Thought and Theology

Artson, Bradley Shavit. *God of Becoming and Relationship: The Dynamic Nature of Process Theology.* Woodstock, VT: Jewish Lights, 2013.

Cobb, John B., and David Ray Griffin. *Process Theology: An Introductory Exposition.* Louisville, KY: Westminster John Knox Press, 1976.

Keller, Catherine. *On the Mystery: Discerning Divinity in Process.* Minneapolis, MN: Fortress Press, 2008.

Mesle, C. Robert. *Process Theology: A Basic Introduction.* St. Louis, MO: Chalice Press, 1993.

Scientific Literacy

Barbour, Ian G. *Religion and Science: Historical and Contemporary Issues.* San Francisco, CA: HarperSanFrancisco, 1997.

Edelman, Gerald M. *Second Nature: Brain Science and Human Knowledge.* New Haven, CT: Yale University Press, 2006.

Gleiser, Marcelo. *The Dancing Universe: From Creation Myths to the Big Bang.* New York: Plume, 1998.

Morowitz, Harold J. *The Emergence of Everything: How the World Became Complex.* Oxford, UK: Oxford University Press, 2002.

Polkinghorne, John. *Quantum Theory: A Very Short Introduction.* Oxford, UK: Oxford University Press, 2002.

Rolston, Holmes. *Science and Religion: A Critical Survey.* Philadelphia, PA: Templeton Foundation Press, 2006.

Smith, Howard, *Let There Be Light: Modern Cosmology and Kabbalah.* Novato, CA: New World Library, 2006.

Smolin, Lee. *Time Reborn: From the Crisis in Physics to the Future of the Universe.* Boston: Mariner Books, 2013.

Putting It All Together

Abrams, Nancy Ellen, and Joel R. Primack. *The New Universe and the Human Future: How a Shared Cosmology Could Transform the World*. New Haven, CT: Yale University Press, 2011.

Chamovitz, Daniel. *What a Plant Knows: A Field Guide to the Senses*. New York: Scientific American, 2012.

Clayton, Philip, and Arthur Peacocke, eds. *In Whom We Live and Move and Have Our Being: Panentheistic Reflections on God's Presence in a Scientific World*. Grand Rapids, MI: William B. Eerdmans, 2004.

Cobb, John B., ed. *Back to Darwin: A Richer Account of Evolution*. Grand Rapids, MI: William B. Eerdmans, 2008.

Narby, Jeremy. *Intelligence in Nature: An Inquiry into Knowledge*. New York: Penguin, 2005.

Noë, Alva. *Out of Our Heads: Why You Are Not Your Brain, and the Other Lessons from the Biology of Consciousness*. New York: Hill and Wang, 2009.

Swimme, Brian, and Thomas Berry. *The Universe Story: From the Primordial Flaring Forth to the Ecozoic Era—A Celebration of the Unfolding of the Cosmos*. New York: HarperOne, 1992.

Printed in the USA
CPSIA information can be obtained
at www.ICGtesting.com
JSHW022341140824
68134JS00019B/1619